Tigers

PETER JACKSON

Eagle Editions

A QUANTUM BOOK

Published by Eagle Editions Ltd
11 Heathfield
Royston
Hertfordshire SG8 5BW

Copyright ©MCMXC
Quintet Publishing plc

This edition printed 2003

ISBN 1-86160-668-0

QUMVAT

This book is produced by
Quantum Publishing Ltd
6 Blundell Street
London N7 9BH

Typeset in Great Britain by
Central Southern Typesetters, Eastbourne
Manufactured in Hong Kong by
Regent Publishing Services Limited

Printed in Singapore by
Star Standard Industries (Pte) Ltd

Tigers

CONTENTS

FOREWORD

As Project Officer of the World Wildlife Fund's 'Operation Tiger' and, subsequently, as Chairman of the Cat Specialist Group of the International Union for Conservation of Nature and Natural Resources (IUCN), it has been my privilege to mix with the scientists and conservationists who have done so much to stem the tide of extinction. In addition, a host of tiger trackers and forest guards have guided me in the jungle haunts of the tiger. My gratitude for their contribution to this book is hereby acknowledged. I should like, in particular, to name Anatoley Bragin, Gui Xiaojie, Ullas Karanth, Paul Leyhausen, Lu Houji, Charles (Chuck) McDougal, Hemanta Mishra, Guy Mountfort, Hemendra Panwar, Prem Bahadur Rai, Ranjitsinh, Fateh Singh Rathore, Kailash Sankhala, George Schaller, Ulysses Seal, John Seidensticker, 'Billy' Arjan Singh, Dave Smith, Mel Sunquist, Kirti Man Tamang, Tan Bangjie, Valmik Thapar, Xiang Peilun and Victor Zhyvotchenko.

Peter Jackson

INTRODUCTIO

As I walked down a forest track in Nepal one day, a tiger stepped from the bushes some distance ahead. I moved quietly behind a tree to watch. The tiger sat down and gazed in my direction. After a while he rose, sniffed a nearby tree, turned to eject scent, and began to walk towards me. About 30 paces away he turned once more into the bushes. My jeep arrived and we drove close to the undergrowth, trying unsuccessfully to spot the tiger. One of my companions suddenly said: 'Look behind!' The tiger was standing again on the track, looking curiously at us. Then he walked on with majestic unconcern.

On another occasion, this time in India, I was on an elephant searching for a tiger whose kill was nearby. We came upon him in a dry river bed, sprawled comfortably on his back in a shady spot, just like a pet cat on the hearth. He raised his head to glance at us, then sank back, closed his eyes and drifted off to sleep. Dappled sunlight illuminated his rich, black-striped, golden fur, his white chest and belly. With a massive paw, he brushed a fly from his nose.

Another time, a tiger emerged from behind a boulder and faced my open jeep. I examined him closely through binoculars. His shoulder muscles

BELOW: Tigers prefer to walk on forest tracks rather than push through the undergrowth. If they meet anyone they usually slip into the bushes. They will not normally attack people unless unexpectedly disturbed.

rippled as though he were about to spring. A shiver of fear ran through me. But he turned and disappeared into the jungle.

I have had many close encounters with tigers, but these incidents illustrate some of their outstanding characteristics: an aloof, self-sufficient air; sheer beauty; and raw power. They left me with a sense of awe. It is impossible to see a tiger in the wild without a quickening of the pulse. Few people in the past had the experience, unless they were actually hunting. A century ago, when tigers were common, a British officer in India, Captain J. Forsyth, confirmed this fact, writing: 'During 10 years of pretty constant roaming about on foot in the most tigerish localities of the Central Provinces (central India), I have only twice come across a tiger when I was not out shooting, and only twice more when I was not actually searching for tigers to shoot'.

Today, anyone with a few days to spare has a good chance of seeing a tiger in the wild, if they go to the right place. The change in behaviour has occurred where tigers are no longer hunted and are losing their fear of humans. But protection has come at the eleventh hour and is far from complete. Poachers are active everywhere, and skins are still clandestinely traded. For the tiger, extinction within a few decades is a real possibility, despite all that conservation efforts have achieved.

There are overwhelming reasons for conserving the tiger and nature in general. Few would question the importance of saving the Abu Simbel Temples in Egypt, the Parthenon in Greece, and other monuments to human genius. Of equal importance are the marvels of nature. The tiger has a right to life on Earth, just as we have. If it is wiped out, it can never be re-created.

ABOVE: Tigers allow a close approach when people go on elephants in several Indian reserves. They do not seem to consider them a threat now that hunting has been abandoned. It sometimes looks as though they are posing for photos.

RIGHT: The Taj Mahal is one of the wonders of the world. People flock to see this white marble tomb of a Moghul empress at Agra. If it were destroyed, human skill could recreate it. Extinction for the tiger would be for ever.

ONE

A
DAY
IN THE
LIFE
OF THE
TIGER

The sun blazes down over the forest. Few birds sing. Most wild animals have taken refuge in the deep shade, but even there the temperature is about 100°C (37°F). Many streams and ponds have dried up, but from a small patch of water that remains, a tiger's head protrudes. His mouth is open and his tongue hangs out. His eyes are dull. All life is at a low ebb. The middle of the day in high summer is a hard time for humans and animals in the tropics, a torment that has to be endured for several months of each year.

Towards late afternoon the sun is sinking to the west and the heat is abating. The tiger yawns, stands up and ploughs through the water to the bank. His coat shines as he steps out. Water drips from his belly and the curve of his tail. Forelegs extended, he stretches and his muscles ripple. Now to hunt for the day's meal.

There are no animals near the pool where the tiger has rested during the day. His presence was all too obvious. But there are other waterholes, and this is the time when the deer, antelope, monkeys and pigs move from the shady

BELOW: A male peacock spreads his ornate tail in a courtship dance before a bevy of females. They appear distinterested, but are sizing him up as a potential mate.

forest to slake their thirst. A troop of grey langur monkeys descends from the trees. They take quick sips of water, frequently raising their heads to look around. Mothers sit with their babies on their laps, and youngsters chase each other. Peacocks strut, spreading the colourful fan of their great tails and dancing before the drab females, who seem unimpressed. A large blue-grey antelope, a nilgai, walks to the water. Birds are singing and all is peaceful.

A sharp, high-pitched bark sounds from among the trees. All the animals around the waterhole look up and freeze. A tense silence reigns. A deer

ABOVE: Tigers advertise their presence by leaving scent marks as they patrol their territories. Other tigers recognise them, and leave their own 'calling cards'.

ABOVE: Watchful
langur monkeys
spot a tiger on the
prowl. Their angry,
gritty calls alert the
other jungle folk.

has sighted the tiger and given warn-
ing that he is on the prowl. Is he
coming to the waterhole? Where is he?
The deer's alarm call rings out again
and others join in the chorus. But then
there is silence and after a time the
animals begin to relax, to drink and
play again.

The tiger is walking openly along a
jungle trail and is easily seen by the
deer. Knowing that he has no chance
of catching any so alert, he ignores their
alarm calls. They watch him pass by,
resuming grazing and browsing as he
disappears. A visible, relaxed tiger is
not to be feared. From time to time he
sniffs at the trunk of a tree or the leaves
of a bush. His mouth opens and his
nose wrinkles as he absorbs the scent.
It is where he scent-marked several
days earlier. He turns, raises his tail,
and squirts a refresher dose, which
will tell other tigers that he has passed
this way and that this is his territory.

Sensitive to the sounds all around,
the tiger's ears turn to focus on those
which might indicate the presence of
unwary prey – the rustle of deer feeding, the snuffling of wild pigs digging
for roots. A troop of langur monkeys
swears grittily at him, but he ignores
them. On a slight rise the tiger halts,
raises his head and looks ahead towards
a small lake, where a herd of sambar
deer is immersed up to their necks as
they feed on the water plants. After
observing them for a while, the tiger
silently slips from the trail and makes
his way through the trees to the tall
grass bordering the lake. There he lies
down in the cover. The deer, now quite
close, continue grazing in the water.
They look round nervously from time

to time, for they know that they are vulnerable to an attack. But all seems quiet and they graze on. The tiger continues to watch them intently from between the stems of grass. His body tenses as one of the deer strays closer to him, a white egret poised upon its back to spot fish. But it moves away all too soon.

The tiger quietly rises and finds another vantage point. Now some spotted deer emerge from the forest nearby. Ears pricked, heads turning to spot any threat, they pick their way cautiously towards the water. Reassured by the peaceful sight of the sambar grazing in the lake, they move to the shore and start to drink. But, still alert, they raise their heads from time to time to look round.

One deer strays from the herd. The tiger eases his hind legs into position to power a spring, forepaws spread firmly on the ground, the tip of his tail twitching. The deer raises its head and looks around, but as it lowers it once more to the water, the tiger charges. The peace of the scene is shattered.

ABOVE: A powerful male tiger, known in Ranthambhore Tiger Reserve as Genghis Khan, stalks sambar as they feed in a lake. With a powerful charge he will try to seize one of them. But many times the prey escapes. Even a tiger often fails.

Animals scatter. The spotted deer dash back to the forest. The sambar swim and leap away desperately through a mass of spray.

The deer targeted by the tiger swerves and starts to run, but manages only a few steps. In an instant the tiger is on it. His long canines clamp on the nape and his powerful claws grasp the skin. His weight drags the deer to the ground. The tiger swiftly changes his grip and goes for the throat, throttling the windpipe in a vice as the deer's legs thrash wildly. Soon the deer only twitches, and finally falls limp. The tiger holds on, his flanks heaving as he regains his breath after the supreme effort.

Meanwhile, forest life has resumed. More spotted deer are drinking further along the lakeside, and the sambar graze in the water at a distant part of the lake. A log-like crocodile glides silently through the still water, eyes, nosetip and ridged tail just protruding. Duck and geese, which had taken off

BELOW: Spotted deer come to drink and graze by the lake. But they seldom relax, knowing that their lives depend on detecting the presence of a tiger.

ABOVE: Gliding
silently through the
water, its back
glistening in the
sunlight, a marsh
crocodile poses
another danger to
deer when they
come to drink.

in panic, have returned to the water after circling several times to check that all is again calm.

The tiger stands up and looks around. Then he bends over the neck of his prey and with a mighty tug starts to drag the 50 kg (110 lb) carcass to the cover of the tall grass. With scissor-like carnassial teeth, the tiger slices off chunks of meat from the deer's hindquarters and swallows them hungrily. He makes a good meal for an hour or two before resting a moment and walk-ing to the lake shore to drink. By now night has fallen, but a full moon bathes the jungle in a soft light.

Already the tiger's flanks, lean before the attack, are swelling from the meal. For the moment he has had enough. He starts to walk around, head swinging low. A distant 'ahouw' brings his head up, ears pricked. It is the roar of another tiger. But after listening intently for a moment, he resumes his stroll and returns to his kill, where he slumps down for a nap.

Tigers use trees as scratching posts (above), just as a house cat uses the furniture. Always on the lookout for carcasses, vultures quickly assemble near a tiger kill (right). They only descend to feed when the tiger is absent.

From time to time during the night he feeds some more, and takes a drink. As the moonlight fades with the dawn, birds sing their greeting. Langur monkeys stir in the trees, hooting softly. Deer are still grazing along the lake, and a sounder of pigs, females accompanied by a horde of little piglets, comes to drink and then trots off again into the grass. The mud is alive with small waders pecking at insects. White egrets stalk the shallows, stabbing at tiny fish.

The tiger decides to go walkabout again. But before leaving he drags grass and leaves over his kill to conceal it from the vultures. Soon they will be drifting overhead, scanning the landscape for carrion. Just as on the previous evening, the tiger walks calmly along old trails and tracks, even roads, checking scent marks and renewing them. He urinates and defecates, scraping the ground with his hind feet. At a strong tree trunk he stands and digs his claws into the bark and tears at it. The action cleans his claws and removes any worn pieces.

Within an hour he is back near the kill – and finds that the vultures have spotted it. Some sit hunched in surrounding trees. Others, noting a congregation that can only mean food, plane down to join them. They drop to the ground and advance on the dead deer, plunging their bare heads into the body. They tear off bits of meat with powerful bills, squabbling and squawking as they fight over the choicest parts.

The sight irritates the tiger, who bares his teeth and angrily flicks his tail. He charges and sends the vultures scattering frantically into the air. His ownership reasserted, he takes a few bites from the kill. By now he is well fed. The heat begins to build up, and he feels sleepy. For a time he settles down near the kill to make sure that the vultures do not return. But the sun grows hotter and he retreats to a shady spot under the trees, where he lolls back and yawns. His eyelids drop and he drifts into sleep. It is a fitful sleep. No animal in the jungle can afford to sleep too deeply. He stirs from time to time, ears twitching, as he checks the sounds around for anything unusual. Then, completely relaxed, he rolls on his back, yawning again, his great paws idly brushing away the flies attracted by the blood on his face.

BELOW: The sight of the vultures eating his kill enrages the tiger. He charges. The vultures, heavy with food, have difficulty in escaping, and the tiger seizes one of them. But he will not eat it, for vulture flesh is repugnant to most other animals.

Thirst awakens him and he ambles down to the lakeside and drinks. The water is cool and refreshing. He turns and backs into it to lie half-submerged for an hour before deciding to have a snack from his kill. Not far away some crocodiles have crawled ashore on to the rocks to warm their cold blood, but as the heat builds up they slip back into the water. White egrets continue to patrol the shallows. Ducks float on the mirror-like water with their bills tucked under their wings. In the heat of the day, peace reigns.

As the afternoon draws on, the tiger starts to come to life. Today he has plenty of food left on the deer carcass. Nevertheless, if an unwary animal passes within striking distance, he will not lose the opportunity to add another meal to his larder. The kill lasts another night, but by the second morning only a few scraps remain and the tiger has gone. That evening the round will start again. Perhaps this time he will detect the scent mark of a tigress advertising her readiness to mate. But that, as Rudyard Kipling said, is another story.

TWO

THE
ORIGIN
AND
SPREAD
OF THE
TIGER

The tiger belongs to the order Carnivora, an order of mammals which evolved primarily as meat-eaters preying on the vegetarian herbivores, and on their own kind. Dogs, bears, racoons, hyenas, otters, weasels, badgers, mongooses and civets are also carnivores. What links them is the possession of carnassial teeth, a pair on each side of the jaws that perform like scissors to slice through meat. However, some carnivores, notably pandas, have become almost wholly vegetarian and their carnassials have become grinding teeth. Other mammals, such as monkeys and apes, as well as humans, will readily eat meat, but they do not possess carnassials.

The carnivores have been traced back to small civet-like animals called *miacids*, which lived more than 65 million years ago in a world dominated by giant reptiles, the dinosaurs. When the dinosaurs vanished, for reasons scientists continue to debate, the miacids lived on to evolve into several hundred species. Of these, well over 200 survive, some immense, such as the polar bear, weighing over a ton. Others, such as the weasel, remain tiny. Of the cats, about 37 species exist today, ranging from the black-footed and the rusty-spotted cats, which are the size of small domestic cats, to lions and tigers, which have been known to weigh over 300 kg (660 lb).

TOP: A jungle cat looks like a house cat as it rests contentedly in the forest.

ABOVE: The deadly canine teeth of a tiger, and the slicing carnassials.

Prehistoric remains of giant cats with long, dagger-like canine teeth have been called sabre-tooth tigers, but they were not progenitors of the tigers we know today. They belonged to a separate branch of cat evolution, which eventually became extinct less than a million years ago. True tigers evolved in eastern Asia. Some of the earliest fossils have been found in Siberia, which is often thought to be where they first appeared. However, there is evidence that the South China tiger could be the stem species from which the eight subspecies of modern times evolved as tigers spread to other regions. China is, in fact, the only country which has been the home of four of these subspecies.

The most complete early tiger-like skull was found in China and named *Felis palaeosinensis*. It is estimated to be more than 2 million years old. At that time, forests covered most of the land of central and southern Asia. Tigers spread westwards through the northern central woodlands and grasslands, following river systems lined by woods and tall grasses to reach as far as the Caspian Sea and eastern Turkey. Others moved south and west into southeast Asia and on to India. Tigers reached the islands of Sumatra, Java and Bali, presumably during the Pleistocene epoch over a million years ago, when sea levels receded and exposed the continental shelf linking the islands with the Malayan peninsula. On the other hand, while they radiated to the very south of India, they did not cross the relatively narrow straits to Sri Lanka, despite their strong swimming ability.

ABOVE: Tiger expert Prem Bahadur Rai demonstrates the tiger's killing bite. The massive skull belonged to a powerful male that dominated the centre of Nepal's Chitwan National Park. He was accidentally drowned.

TIGER DISTRIBUTION ± 1900

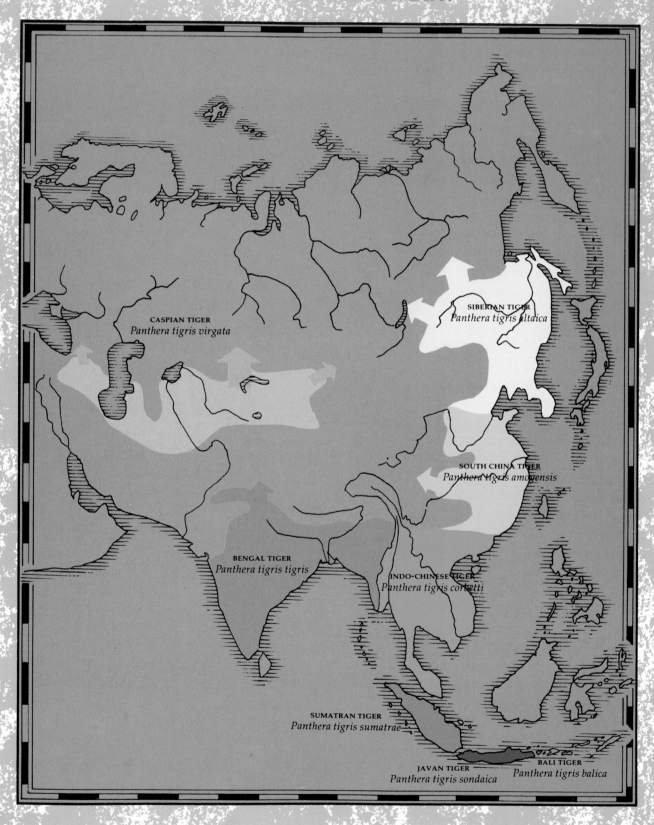

CASPIAN TIGER
Panthera tigris virgata

SIBERIAN TIGER
Panthera tigris altaica

SOUTH CHINA TIGER
Panthera tigris amoyensis

BENGAL TIGER
Panthera tigris tigris

INDO-CHINESE TIGER
Panthera tigris corbetti

SUMATRAN TIGER
Panthera tigris sumatrae

JAVAN TIGER
Panthera tigris sondaica

BALI TIGER
Panthera tigris balica

When the great Swedish taxonomist, Carl Linné, known by the Latinized name Linnaeus, established the modern classification of animals, his type specimen in 1758 was a tiger from Bengal, which in those days was the name for northern and eastern India. Linnaeus classified the tiger as *Felis tigris*, *Felis* being the genus containing cat species. Later scientists put the tiger into a separate genus, called *Panthera*, because it has elastic sections on either side of the hyoid bone (which supports the tongue), unlike the smaller cats, whose hyoid is solid bone. Lions, leopards, jaguars and snow leopards also have elastic hyoids and are included in the genus *Panthera*. The elasticity has long been considered the root of the ability to roar, an attribute common to all members of the genus *Panthera*, except the snow leopard. But recent studies by an American otolaryngologist, Dr Malcolm Hast, have shown that the roaring cats have a large mass of fibro-elastic tissue at the top of very large, undivided vocal folds. Combined with the elastic hyoid, the vocal apparatus acts like a valve trumpet or a slide trombone and efficiently radiates the sound as a roar. Only the snow leopard lacks the laryngeal pad, which explains why it does not roar. The elastic hyoid allows the big cats to purr only when they breathe out. Other cats purr when breathing both in and out.

The tiger is a superbly equipped predator, with the power to take animals much larger than itself. Its long canine teeth in both jaws are the killing weapons, which clamp on to the prey. The carnassials, at the sides of

the jaws, facilitate feeding by slicing flesh. Tigers walk on their forepads and toes. This gives a spring to their gait lacking in flat-footed animals, such as bears. The paws have strong claws, which remain retracted until extended to seize prey. As with other cats, except the cheetah, the tiger has flexible forelegs which it can twist inwards, thus enabling it to grasp.

Tigers possess acute hearing and vision. Their forward-facing eyes provide binocular vision, which makes it

ABOVE: Half hidden in the bushes, a tiger sizes up its prey. Silently, it moves its hind legs into position to power a devastating charge to bring it down. Tigers have to get close to a potential prey to catch it; speed is essential if nimble animals are not to escape.

RIGHT: Tigers' eyes shine in a spotlight.

BELOW: Tigers grimace when they sniff scentmarks of other tigers.

possible to judge direction and distance. The pupils are round, compared with the vertical slits in most small cats. As other cats, tigers have cone cells in their eyes as well as rods, implying that they have colour vision. Many mammals, which possess only rods, see in monochrome. Experiments suggest that domestic cats do not normally make serious use of colour vision, but no one knows whether tigers do. They are certainly very sensitive to movement, a vital attribute in jungle life.

A most important attribute of a tiger is the ability to see in the dark. A tiger's vision is about the same as a human being's in daylight, but six times better at night. All cats, and some other species, possess an adaptation to the retina called the *tapetum lucidum*, which reflects light back through the retina, and in doing so doubles the intensity of dim light. This feature also accounts for the way cats' eyes shine when a light is focused on them at night.

Dogs are renowned for their sense of smell, which guides most of their

CURRENT DISTRIBUTION

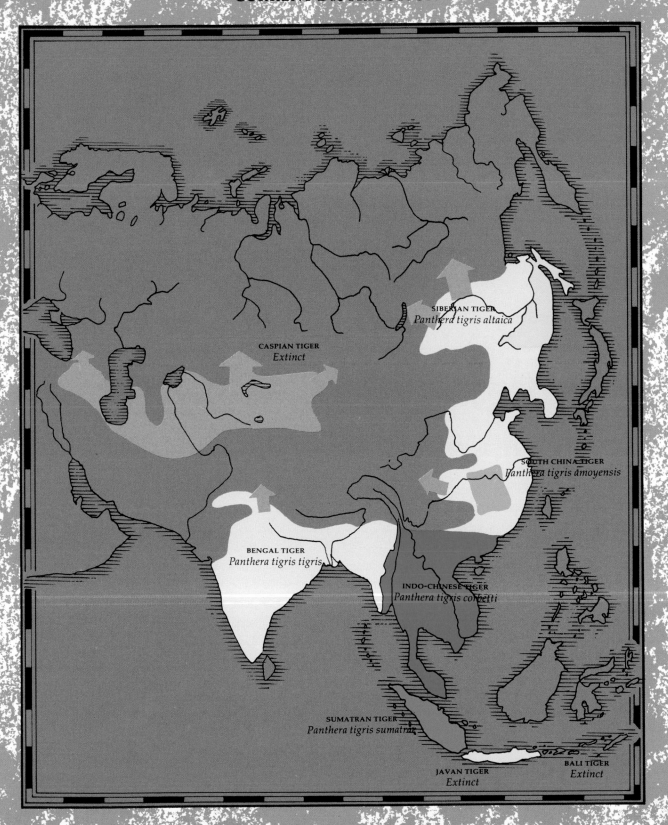

SIBERIAN TIGER
Panthera tigris altaica

CASPIAN TIGER
Extinct

SOUTH CHINA TIGER
Panthera tigris amoyensis

BENGAL TIGER
Panthera tigris tigris

INDO-CHINESE TIGER
Panthera tigris corbetti

SUMATRAN TIGER
Panthera tigris sumatrae

JAVAN TIGER
Extinct

BALI TIGER
Extinct

activity. Tigers have been seen sniffing when tracking prey, but they do not follow a scent trail as a dog does. Nevertheless, scent-marking is a key social activity by which cats, including tigers, maintain contact and send messages to their kind. The fluid is ejected from the urinary channel, but carries secretions from anal glands. Tigers mark their territory continually, checking the signs left by themselves or others and re-marking. These scent marks alert other tigers to the marker's presence, and probably indicate something about the animal's age and condition. A tigress in heat advertises her readiness for mating by marking frequently. The scent informs males of her condition so that they seek her out. She will also give distinctive moaning roars, which tell males where she is.

When sniffing a scent mark, tigers wrinkle their noses and hang out their tongues in a peculiar grimace, which has been given the German name *flehmen*. Although it looks like a gesture of distaste, this is the way the scent is drawn to a sensitive organ in the roof of the mouth, known as 'Jacobson's organ', which is presumed to interpret the information. The scent is probably also embedded in the faeces. Unlike domestic cats, which usually bury their faeces, tigers often leave them in prominent places to make their presence known.

ABOVE: The Indo-Chinese tiger closely resembles the Bengal tiger. The scientific name *corbetti* honours a famous British hunter of man-eaters in India. The range is from Burma through continental southeast Asia.

ABOVE: The South China tiger has been hunted to the very brink of extinction. Fewer than 50 are believed to survive.

Tigers vary in head and body length from 1.4 m (4.6 ft) to 2.8 m (9.2 ft). The tail measures another 0.6–0.95 m (2.0–3.1 ft). Males are considerably larger and more bulky than females and grow a ruff of hair round the neck.

As tigers dispersed from their point of origin, they adapted to the local environments. Populations isolated from other tiger groups evolved into subspecies, distinguished by unique features. The Siberian tiger, *Panthera tigris altaica*, is the heaviest subspecies. Weights of up to 306 kg (675 lb) have been recorded. The Russian naturalist, Nikolai Baikov, declared that males had been found with a length of 3.9 m (12.8 ft), including the tail of 1 m (3.3 ft). Other records give an average length of about 3 m (9.8 ft). The muzzle is broader than in other tiger subspecies, and the head and forequarters are massive. The coat is distinctively pale and the stripes brown rather than black. In winter the fur grows long and shaggy.

The Siberian tiger is also known as the Amur tiger, from the river in the centre of its range which forms the boundary of China and the Soviet Far East, and as the Manchurian tiger. Its range once extended from the Sea of Okhotsk to Lake Baikal and well into northern China. Today it is confined to the Primorye (Maritime) Province, north of Vladivostok, with a small number just across the border in China, where it is known as the Northeast China tiger.

Bengal tigers, *Panthera tigris tigris*, may reach the same length as Siberian specimens, but they are less massive. Their coats vary from a lightish yellow to reddish yellow and their stripes are black. Hunters in India claimed to have shot huge tigers as long as 3.5 m (11.5 ft), but these records are suspect. There was considerable competition to shoot the biggest tiger, and measurements are likely to have been exaggerated. A leading naturalist in India, the late E.P. Gee, noted that tigers of this size were usually shot by British viceroys, when they were guests of a maharajah. But skins were sometimes stretched, and measuring tapes of 11 inches to the foot were rumoured to have been used.

Formerly, the Bengal tiger roamed all the forested areas of the Indian subcontinent and the reedbeds of the Indus River in what is now Pakistan. Today it is extinct in Pakistan and survives in small, scattered populations in India, Nepal, Bangladesh and Burma. Its total number is estimated at about 6,000, compared with a possible 40,000 at the turn of the century. The largest single population, which may number more than 500, is in the coastal mangrove forests of the Sundarbans in eastern India and Bangladesh.

The Indo-Chinese tiger, *Panthera tigris corbetti*, was scientifically described as a separate subspecies from the Bengal tiger only in 1968, on the grounds that it is smaller and darker, and has stripes that are short, narrow, and rarely doubled. The Irrawaddy River in Burma was suggested as the division between the two subspecies, with the Indo-Chinese tiger's range running through Thailand, Malaysia and Indo-China, and into southern China. The total population is unknown, but could be over 2,000. Malaysian authorities estimate that there are 600 tigers in the peninsula, and a figure of 500 has been suggested for Thailand. That leaves vast areas of forest in Burma and Indo-China, where Indo-Chinese tigers still exist and could easily number 1,000.

The South China tiger, *Panthera tigris amoyensis*, gets its Latin name from the island of Amoy, from where skins used to be exported. It once ranged throughout the heart of China, mainly to the south of the Yangtse River. Today, Chinese scientists believe that fewer than 50 survive, mostly in the mountainous regions bordering Hunan Province. This subspecies is also smaller than the Bengal tiger, and the stripes are short, broad and less numerous.

No recent trace has been found of the Caspian tiger, *Panthera tigris virgata*, and it is considered extinct. It was once found in eastern Turkey, Iran, northern Iraq, on both sides of the Caspian Sea in the USSR, particularly along the Amu Darya and Syr Darya rivers, and in Afghanistan. About the same size as the Bengal tiger, the Caspian tiger had longer, narrower and more numerous stripes, which were not fully black. It had long cheek whiskers and longish hair on the neck.

The Sumatran tiger, *Panthera tigris sumatrae*, is smaller than the Bengal tiger. Its coat is darker and more

RIGHT: Some tigers carry a gene which produces white fur, brown stripes and blue eyes. Litters may contain both normal and white cubs.

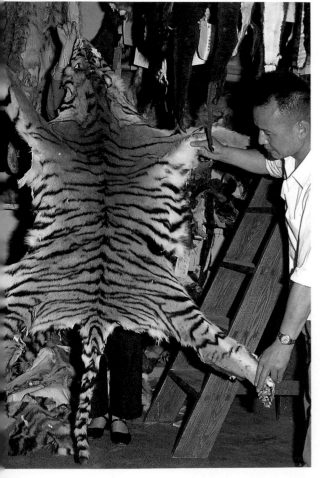

reddish-ochre, with broad, black stripes, which are often doubled. Although tigers are still found throughout the island, their number is unknown. Estimates have put the figure at about 1,000. Poaching is widespread, with skins being smuggled out, especially to nearby Singapore.

Two more subspecies, the Javan tiger, *Panthera tigris sondaicus,* and the Bali tiger, *P. tigris balica,* are almost certainly extinct. Reports of survivors occur from time to time, but investigation has usually shown the animals involved to be leopards or other cats. Males of these two subspecies weighed only 90–100 kg (198–220 lb) and were even darker in colour than the Sumatran tiger. The Javan tiger had numerous, close-set stripes. The Bali tiger had fewer stripes and was the darkest subspecies.

There were still tigers in several parts of Java after World War II, but this is one of the most densely populated and cultivated areas in the world, and by the 1970s tigers were only known in the extreme southeast of the island, in and around the Meru Betiri Reserve. A careful survey in 1980 found tracks of at least three tigers, but there has been no sign since.

Bali tigers were still being shot in the 1930s, and some may have survived into the 1940s. Reports of tigers have continued ever since, without ever securing hard evidence. Doubt has been expressed about its validity as a subspecies, although recognized as such by science in 1912. There are suggestions that it may have been introduced to Bali. It is also possible that Javan tigers could have swum the narrow strait, only 2.5 km (1.5 miles) wide, separating Bali from Java.

Odd variations in coat colour and pattern occur in many animals. White tigers are now famous. Since early in the nineteenth century there were reports of white tigers, mainly in the forests of central India. In 1951, the maharajah of Rewa caught a nine-month-old white cub in the Band-havghar Forests. He took it to his palace zoo and named it Mohan. When Mohan reached maturity, he was mated with a normal-coloured tigress named Begum from the same forests. Begum produced three litters totalling 10 cubs, all of the normal reddish-orange colour.

Mohan was then mated with one of his daughters, Radha, and in 1958 she gave birth to four white cubs, one male and three females. While the maharajah kept Mohan until his death in 1969, the Delhi Zoo became the main breeding centre for white tigers. Some were exported and led to the production of white tigers in zoos and circuses in Europe and North America. Another white strain appeared in the USA when a pure-bred Siberian tiger produced white cubs when mated with a normal-coloured tiger of unknown ancestry at the Hawthorn Circus in Illinois. A second white Siberian tiger was born at Center Hill in Florida. In India, a white Bengal tiger was produced at Nandankanan Zoo by a pair not known to be related to Mohan.

White tigers are not albinos, which lack dark pigments. Their eyes are blue, not pink, and their stripes are brown or black. The white coat is the result of a recessive gene, which takes effect when two carriers mate. This explains why father-daughter matings produce white offspring. Litters often include both white and normal-coloured cubs.

Unfortunately, the inbreeding involved in building up the numbers of white tigers has had genetic effects, so that fertility has declined. Litters have been smaller, and a high percentage of cubs have died. White tigers have often had eye problems and are susceptible to pneumonia, feline distemper, lung congestion and abdominal problems. A controlled breeding programme mating white and normal-coloured tigers could probably overcome these problems.

Mohan was the last known wild white tiger. The possibility of reintroducing the white genes to the wild has been proposed, but geneticists are not in favour of it, because of the defects which have developed among captives.

Some cats, notably leopards and jaguars, produce black or melanistic specimens, but scientists have not found any black tigers. Nevertheless, there have been reports of their existence. One, said to have been shot in the eighteenth century in southern India (a likely humid tropical forest habitat where black leopards are found), was painted by an East India Company employee. The painting still existed in 1964, but was later sold to an unknown buyer as part of a collection. Several other reports of black tigers in

India appear to have concerned black leopards. The possibility of black tigers cannot be ruled out, but there is little chance that examples still exist, since there are few tigers in India now, and they live in relatively well-surveyed habitats.

A blue tiger was reported from Fujian, China (in the range of the South China tiger), by American hunter Harry R. Caldwell in 1910. He described its appearance at a goat bait he had put out and wrote that it was 'a deep shade of maltese (ie like the blue of the domestic Maltese cat), changing into almost deep blue on the underparts'. The stripes were normal. It disappeared before he could shoot it. He said that people claimed to have seen other blue tigers in the area. But appearances can be deceptive and it cannot be excluded that these unique dark tigers had just been rolling in the mud.

ABOVE: Muddy tigers may have led to reports of blue or black tigers.

RIGHT: Black leopards are usually found in dense tropical rain forests. The spots can still be seen under the dark sheen.

THREE

TERRITORY, MATING AND FAMILY LIFE

Tigers mark their passage as they travel through their territories. They spray their scent (right) onto the trunks of trees, leaving a distinctive odour detectable by people. They also leave prominent scratch marks (below). These marks inform other tigers about their presence. A female's readiness to mate is advertised by her scent.

will have a favoured home range, where it spends most of its time.

Tiger territories are not necessarily exclusive. Overlapping occurs. In Siberia, where tigers need to cover vast distances in search of prey, there is considerable overlap. Several tigers follow the same trails at different times. They will know of each other's passage from the scent marks.

Male tigers control territories which may be three times bigger than those of females. While they are aggressive towards other males, they allow females within their territories because they are potential mates. For a tigress, a territory is a place to raise her cubs. She must have sufficient prey within easy access and places to hide her young. A male's territory will usually encompass those of one or two females. One unusually large and powerful tiger in Nepal's Royal Chitwan National Park covered the territories of seven females.

Adult tigers are basically solitary animals. They establish their own territories containing adequate prey, cover and water to support them. In India and Nepal, where prey density is high, male tiger territories extend from 50 to 1,000 km^2 (20 to 386 sq. miles). In eastern Siberia, prey is more widely dispersed and territories range from 500 to 4,000 km^2 (200 to 1,500 sq. miles). But the extent of a territory is also influenced by the power, or lack of power, of the tiger in its relations with its neighbours. Prime territories are held by the strongest tigers, and damaging fights may erupt between near equals. Within its territory a tiger

As they patrol their domains, covering 10–20 km (16–32 miles) in a night, tigers are constantly alert for signs of what is happening around them. They need to know what other tigers are doing. They scent-mark trees and bushes along their route, especially when they detect the scent of another tiger. Tigers make scrape marks with their hind feet alongside a track, and urinate or leave droppings at the spot. Droppings may be left in prominent places, such as the middle of a road. Scratch marks are made on tree trunks, a sign which may have developed from cleaning the claws.

But it is the scent which carries the most information. A tiger can tell whether a scent mark belongs to a familiar local resident or a stranger, a male or a female. A stranger is most likely to be a transient, and therefore less threatening than a neighbour, who may be encroaching on territory. Scent-marking is the main challenge over territory. In the last resort there may be a fight. It seldom leads to death, for the loser retreats. Once superiority is established, the dominant tiger may tolerate the presence of the other animal in part of its range, particularly if it is of the same clan.

A tiger is extremely mobile and may visit each part of its territory every 10 days. It has to follow prey animals, which constantly move when an active

ABOVE: Domestic cats hide their droppings, but tigers often leave them in prominent places. They serve to mark the tiger's territory.

LEFT: During the few days a tigress is in heat, tigers copulate frequently. Immediately after the climax, the tigress whips round, lashing out at her mate, who has to leap clear.

tiger disturbs them. At the same time, the male tiger knows from scent marks whether a tigress within his territory is ready to mate. Her roars, too, will attract him.

In tropical climates, where temperature fluctuations are small, tigresses may come into oestrus throughout the year. In temperate regions, this happens only seasonally. However, mating appears to be more frequent in cooler seasons, even in tropical regions. Zoo records indicate that the period between oestrus is around 50 days.

RIGHT: During mating, the tiger grips his mate firmly by the nape. But his powerful canine teeth do not injure her.

The tigress's calls are answered by the male's roars as they approach each other. If several males are attracted, there may be fights until one has established his superiority. Left to themselves, the mating pair circle each other, growling. At first, the tigress may show some reluctance, and the male has to pursue her. But eventually they rub faces and bodies, and the tigress lies down, raising her tail to one side to allow the male to mount her. He grasps the loose skin of her nape in his jaws. Coupling, which lasts only 15–30 seconds, is accompanied by soft growling and mewing sounds. At the climax the tigress roars, whips round and lashes out at the tiger, who has to leap clear to avoid injury. She rolls voluptuously on her back while the tiger watches. He may lie down for a while before approaching her again. She immediately receives him. Mating occurs frequently – every 15–20 minutes at a peak – for five or six days. Towards the end, the tiger tires, and the tigress has to nudge him into activity by rubbing herself against him and presenting herself. Finally they part. The frequent copulations, common to all the cats, are necessary to induce ovulation in the female.

Gestation takes about 100 days. The tigress seeks secure cover to bear her cubs. She may find a cave or a rock overhang, a hollow tree, or dense vegetation. Up to five or six cubs may be born, but more commonly three or four. All are dropped close together on a mattress of trampled grass. Births observed in captivity were at intervals of 10–20 minutes. The tigress licks each cub clean, and eats the placenta, cord and sac, from which she obtains nourishment. The cubs, blind, fumble their way to the tigress's teats and begin their first feed. Their weight at this time is not more than 1.5 kg (3.3 lb).

The membrane covering the eyes at birth splits when the cubs are about one week old, but they do not see clearly until they have reached two months. By then they are beginning to eat meat brought back by the tigress and have reached a weight of about 10 kg (22 lb). By the time they are five or six months old they have been weaned. In the meantime the tigress is likely to have moved them several times to new dens, carrying them gently, one by one, in her powerful jaws. It is an anxious time for her. While she is out hunting, the young are vulnerable to predators. Leopards, hyenas, jackals, and even male tigers, may all kill and eat tiger cubs.

Cubs are very playful and affectionate. From early on they return the caresses of their mother, rubbing against her face and flanks and climbing over her. Sometimes she cuffs them. They show a hunting instinct by stalking and leaping on each other and attacking their mother's flicking tail. Birds, insects and other small animals are carefully investigated and stalked.

When the cubs are about six months old, the tigress takes them to her kills to feed directly from morsels she has picked off, but she is nervously wary. At any sign of an intruder she signals the cubs to retreat to cover. She may even display herself to divert attention from the cubs. At this stage there is no permanent den and the cubs follow

their mother as she searches for prey. At a kill the cubs already show a 'pecking' order. The strongest monopolizes the choicest portions. It may take all of a small kill. Male cubs take precedence over the females.

Now begins a year of training during which the cubs learn how to live in the jungle. At first they are spectators, watching their mother from cover as she stalks and attacks prey animals. Tigresses have been seen to cripple a deer or buffalo and then allow the cubs to finish it off. From a clumsy start skill soon develops. By the time they are a year old the cubs can successfully tackle deer, pigs and cattle.

During their second year the cubs begin to match their mother in size. At

18 months a male may already be bigger than she is. One or two of the litter may have died of disease or been killed by another predator. Since the ratio of male to female cubs at birth appears to be about equal on average, but adult females outnumber males, it is clear that male cubs are more vulnerable, probably because they are more adventurous. Lacking experience, they may be killed when tackling dangerous prey, such as wild boar, buffalo and gaur (wild ox). Packs of wild dogs also kill tigers, and young ones are easily overcome.

Only one or two of a litter generally survive the first two years of life. Tigresses have been seen with four full-grown cubs, but this is most

unusual. Gradually, the cubs show more independence, until, by the age of 18 to 20 months, a male will leave to seek his own territory. Females stay longer with their mother.

The father plays no part in the upbringing of the cubs, and it has often been suggested that he may be a danger to them. But recent observations show that a close relationship can endure. In the Ranthambhore Tiger Reserve, about 200 km (125 miles) southwest of Delhi, strict protection over the past 15 years has encouraged some tigers to ignore human observers and behave naturally in the open in daylight. Thus, two tiger specialists, Fateh Singh Rathore and Valmik Thapar, were able to observe a tigress and cubs affectionately greeting a male, thought to be the father. Another male was seen to visit two families, both presumed to be his.

On another occasion, Thapar and Rathore saw nine tigers lying together, just like a pride of lions. In Kanha National Park, in central India, a family gathering included year-old cubs and their mother, one of her sons from a previous litter and the presumed father. Tiger groups have also been observed sharing a kill, with the male taking precedence.

Russian scientists believe that some tigers form relatively stable social groups when they are unable to estab-

LEFT: All jungle animals, including tigers, fear the red dogs. They hunt in packs, which run down prey and tear it to pieces in a few minutes.

lish home ranges of their own, live in areas where prey is scarce, and lack females with which to mate. In eastern Siberia, they have found tracks of parties of five to seven tigers repeatedly moving together.

Such assemblies do not, however, disprove the solitary nature of the tiger when compared with the lion. The different habitats in which they evolved and live encouraged their divergent lifestyles. Lions live mainly in open habitats where there is abundant prey, and social units, based on mother-daughter relationships, survive through cooperative hunting. But cooperation is no advantage for the tiger hunting in dense cover, where prey is dispersed and rare. Even lions tend to become more solitary in areas where there are no large concentrations of prey.

The young male tiger faces the most challenging time of his life when he leaves his mother. He is not powerful enough to wrest territory from mature males and avoids confrontations as he explores the forest. Mature males have been seen to tolerate a subordinate, probably related, male in their territories. Most young males, however,

ABOVE: Unlike the basically solitary tigers, lions are highly social animals, living in prides of females and cubs, with a few mature males.

have to find prey in the less favourable areas as they bide their time until they can gain a territory of their own.

Age and injury eventually weaken all tigers. Thus the young male is able, as he grows stronger, to take over a territory containing tigresses with whom he can mate. He still has to establish the boundaries with his neighbours. Ageing and injured tigers become vagrants if they can no longer hold a territory, and they are forced into the peripheral areas.

Young females also leave their mother to find territories. By then, the tigress will be ready to mate again and will become aggressive towards her cubs. Sometimes, she allows one of her female cubs to settle in part of her

RIGHT: The favoured prey of a tiger is usually a large deer. But small animals are often eaten. In the mangrove delta of the Sundarbans, in India and Bangladesh, even mudskipper fish fall prey to the tiger.

BELOW: Crabs need to duck swiftly into their holes in the sand when a tiger strolls along the beach. He may slap them with a heavy paw and eat them in one gulp.

territory. When that daughter becomes sexually mature, some time after she is about three years old, she is likely to mate with her father. The other female cubs will make their homes within the territories of neighbouring males.

During a lifetime a tigress may have several mates. The best known of all wild tigresses was Chuchchi – a name meaning 'Pointed Toes', given to her by Nepalese trackers in the Royal Chitwan National Park. She was found dead in August 1987 with a broken back, apparently killed by a young male, at an estimated age of 15 years. Scientists who had closely followed her for most of her life noted that seven successive males had had territories overlapping hers. She produced at least 16 cubs in five litters between

1975 and 1985, of which eight survived beyond two years of age.

Tigers eat almost anything that moves, including other tigers on rare occasions. Most-favoured prey are deer and wild boar, which provide substantial meals. But in the coastal mangrove forests of the Sundarbans in India and Bangladesh, they eat fish, frogs and crabs, as well as the giant monitor lizards. Peafowl and monkeys are commonly killed for food. Elephants and rhinoceroses may be taken when young, but as adults they are dangerous adversaries. Tigers are not above scavenging. Like domestic cats, they eat grass, which is believed to have digestive or medicinal effects. Fruits and berries have also been found in tiger droppings.

Given an unexpected opportunity, a tiger will rush and kill any animal unwary enough to pass nearby. But the usual method of catching prey is for the tiger to stalk to within a short distance, aided by the camouflage of its striped coat, and to charge the unsuspecting animal from the rear. Small prey may be killed by a neck bite. The nape of larger animals is also grasped in the jaws, but once they are pulled down, the tiger goes for the throat and throttles the prey.

The immense power of a tiger is demonstrated when it drags or carries off heavy prey, such as a buffalo weighing 200 kg (450 lb), to feed in cover. It starts to eat at the rump. The entrails are dragged out and either eaten or discarded. A tiger may eat

ABOVE: A tiger may consume 20–30 kg (44–66 lb) of meat from one kill. In between meals they drink and rest. Very little is left.

ABOVE: A well-fed tiger dreams away the hot hours in the bamboo jungle of the Kanha National Park. In the late afternoon, he will start a new search for prey, if he has eaten all his kill.

20–30 kg (44–66 lb) at a stretch, and leave very few remains, if undisturbed.

Feeding on a large kill goes on intermittently for two or three days. In between meals the tiger goes to drink and rests nearby. It may go for a stroll – and kill another animal if the opportunity arises. Instinctively, a tiger tries to hide its kill, pulling grass and leaves over it. One was seen pushing small rocks and stones on to its kill in the absence of grass.

Supreme predator the tiger may be, but many times it is unsuccessful in its attacks. The prey may spot the stalking tiger, or sprint away from the final charge. The tiger will not enter a long chase. A big sambar stag attacked by a

tiger may still manage to drag itself free and escape.

Powerful prey animals are capable of injuring and killing tigers when they are attacked. But the tiger has most to fear from wild dogs only one-tenth of its weight. Hunting in packs as large as 30, Asiatic wild dogs or dholes are remorseless hunters, which pursue and tear a living prey to pieces. A tiger may kill and wound some of the pack, but still be doomed.

In the wild, the life of a tiger is brief. The average lifespan is probably not more than 15 years. In the protected environment of zoos, tigers have lived for 16–18 years. One Siberian tiger died at the age of 26.

Lions, once a royal symbol, are now rare in India. But the secretive leopard survives, not only in reserves, but even close to settlements.

igers live in the oak and pine forests of Siberia; in the dry deciduous forests of the Indian sub-continent; in the steamy jungles of southeast Asia; in coastal mangroves; and in grasslands beside rivers. All these habitats contain the green plants that feed the tiger's prey and provide it with cover. Provided there is water too, the tiger is at home.

Several other large predators take similar prey to the tiger. Although there is overlap, each species has its favoured prey, based largely on size. Closest to the tiger is another big cat, the leopard. It is smaller than the tiger and is subordinate in the predator 'pecking order'. Leopards are agile tree climbers, and are powerful enough to haul a 50 kg (110 lb) deer into a tree to keep it safe from other predators. Tigers drive leopards off kills, attack them, and even eat them. Not sur-prisingly, leopards avoid tigers and are normally less common where there are many tigers. However, an unusual association between a male leopard and a tigress was once seen by a hunter in India. Twice the leopard killed a buffalo bait, and was then joined by the tigress for the meal. On a third occasion, the leopard had difficulty in killing the buffalo, and the tigress jumped in and made the kill. They ate together, and were then shot. It was speculated that there might have been a sexual attraction behind the associa-tion. But this is unlikely in the wild, although, in captivity, leopards and tigers may interbreed and produce young.

Leopards are found throughout the range of the tiger. But they also extend to Africa, where the tiger has never existed. Their spots and rosettes equal the camouflage of the tiger, breaking up their outline in the light and shade of the forest. The barest minimum of cover is required by leopards, and they are far more rarely seen than tigers. They often live close to human habita-tion, and will prey on domestic dogs.

BELOW: An Asiatic lioness stalks her prey in the Gir forest, in western India. Her ancestors roamed as far east as eastern Greece in ancient times. About 230 lions in the Gir are the last survivors in Asia.

Lions once lived in northern and central India, the eastern extent of a range which in former times included Iran, Palestine and Greece. The only lions outside Africa now are in the Gir Forest of western India, where there are about 230. Nevertheless, the lion outshone the tiger as a symbol, and, despite its rarity, the national crest of India even today consists of four lions forming the capital of a column erected by the Emperor Ashoka 2,000 years ago. The decline of the lion in India has been attributed to competition with a superior tiger. In fact, they could seldom have met, for their habitats differ, the lion living in relatively open country. Ruthless hunting, especially by British soldiers and administrators during the nineteenth century, brought the Asiatic lion to the very edge of extinction by the turn of the century. Last-minute protection by the ruler of Junagadh State ensured the survival of the small population that exists today.

Several small cats share jungles with tigers. From northeast India through southeast Asia, there are forests containing five or six species – clouded leopard, golden cat, leopard cat, marbled cat, fishing cat and jungle cat.

The rusty-spotted cat, which is smaller than the average domestic cat, and the lynx-like caracal are found in some western areas of India. All live very secretive lives, preying on small mammals, birds and reptiles.

Striped hyenas do not compete with tigers, but may profit from their kills. They share jungles with tigers only in the Indian subcontinent, and no further eastwards. Hyenas live solitary lives in more open country than most tigers, but they overlap in the lighter forests. Hyenas feed on carrion, although they do also kill small mammals themselves. They have exceptionally powerful jaws, adapted to crushing bones. A hyena will feed on an unguarded tiger kill, but retreat quickly if the tiger reappears. They may, however, stand up to leopards, even driving them from their kills.

Jackals also scavenge tiger prey. They have been heavily hunted for their fur and are now less common. But the howling chorus of a pack of jackals can still be heard, sometimes even in towns. Small mammals and birds make up most of the jackal's food. Although they live in packs, they are more often seen in pairs, trotting lightly on their hunt for prey. They are ancestors of domestic dogs, and do not deserve the scorn their name evokes.

A more powerful predator than the jackal, and feared by the tiger, is the Asiatic wild dog, or dhole. They have evoked intense hatred among people because of the way packs tear apart live prey. Their extermination has been called for. Nevertheless, they are part of jungle life throughout the range of the tiger. Wild dogs are handsome animals, with rich reddish chestnut coats and black, bushy tails.

Deer are the principal tiger prey. Several species share the tiger's habitat. Their short, sharp alarm calls when they spot a tiger warn all the jungle inhabitants. If a tiger attacks, they will scatter wildly. But when a relaxed tiger passes, they will watch warily, giving their alarm call and betraying their tension by stamping a forefoot.

An unusual spotted form of the golden cat (above), which lives in thick forests in southern China. The clouded leopard (right) is also a forest animal. Its range is from India into southeast Asia and China.

ABOVE: Striped
hyenas are solitary
animals, which live
in fairly open
country. They may
feed on tiger kills,
but quickly retreat if
the tiger reappears.
They can crunch big
bones with their
exceptionally
powerful jaws.

The most widespread and the largest deer in the tiger's world is the sambar, a relative of the European red deer and the American elk. Stags grow magnificent antlers, and, with a weight of 200–300 kg (440–660 lb), they are bigger than many tigers. Despite their size – or, perhaps, because of it – sambar are favourite prey, providing food for several days for a tiger or for a tigress and cubs. Sambar generally live in the forests, but at Ranthambhore Tiger Reserve in western India, they emerge to feed on water plants in the lakes. In eastern Siberia and north-eastern China, tigers prey on a related species, the maral or Siberian wapiti.

Cheetal, or spotted deer, are confined to the Indian subcontinent. They are much smaller than sambar, but still provide tigers with an ample meal. They live in forests, coming out to graze in herds in the meadows. One of the most beautiful of deer, they have been taken to many parts of the world, where they live in parks and, sometimes, in the wild. In the cooler regions of China and the Soviet Far East, the somewhat similar sika deer is found.

The red dog, or
'dhole' (above), is a
fierce but handsome
animal.
The forest deer of
Asia, known as
'sambar' (right), is a
close relative of the
European red deer
and the American
elk. It is favourite
tiger prey.

Swamp deer, which stand as high as sambar, but are lighter in build, generally inhabit marshy areas, as their name implies. Their hooves spread to support them on the soft ground. In Kanha National Park in central India, a subspecies is found on hard ground. It has evolved close-knit hooves and is renowned for its magnificent 12-point antlers, which form a lofty crown. Twenty years ago the Kanha swamp deer were reduced to fewer than 100 individuals, and tigers were blamed for the decline. Research established that humans were at fault. Official grass burning, designed to improve the habitat, was being carried out just when the fawns needed cover to hide from predators. A change in the grass-burning time has resulted in a dramatic increase in swamp deer numbers.

One of the few animals that will stand up to a tiger is the wild boar, a close

The central Indian swamp deer (above) has magnificent antlers.

Spotted deer (left) manage to survive even in the saline mangroves of the Sundarbans, on the shore of the Bay of Bengal.

Most elephants (above) are too big to be killed by tigers, but babies are vulnerable. Wild boar (right) put up a strong fight if attacked.

relative of the European wild boar. They live in packs called 'sounders', which may have 30 to 40 members. Wild boar are extremely intelligent animals, and can be very aggressive. Tigers and leopards will retreat before an angry wild boar, whose sharp tusks can cause deadly wounds. Even so, wild boar do fall prey to tigers.

In the cut and thrust of jungle life, look-outs play an important role. In India, they are the grey langur monkeys. With black faces, rimmed by grey fur, and long curving tails, langurs are very handsome monkeys, whose food consists mainly of leaves, buds and fruits. Their normal call is a repeated, booming, low hoot. When they break into a chorus of sharp, gritty alarm calls, all the jungle animals know there is a tiger nearby. Langurs can get caught on the ground by tigers, and in the trees by leopards. Cheetal deer are often found below trees in which troops of langurs are feeding. They benefit from the alarm calls of the monkeys.

Many small animals may visit an untended tiger kill. Lively mongooses delicately eat the flesh. Porcupines come to gnaw bones, but at the risk of attack by the tiger. Their sharp quills, however, are dangerous, and tigers often suffer severe, even crippling, wounds.

Peafowl fall prey to tigers. Turkey-sized, they make a good meal. During the wet season, peacocks may often be seen performing their spectacular mating dance with their magnificent tail coverts spread in a great arc. Alarm calls from deer and monkeys halt the display. When the tiger appears the peafowl take off with harsh screams. As the evening light dims, they take refuge in the trees until dawn.

Drifting in leisurely fashion in the skies over the jungles are the vultures, ever alert for assemblies of their kind that denote a carcass on which to feed. Dozens will scramble hungrily over a tiger kill – when the tiger is absent. While the tiger feeds, they stay safely in the trees, awaiting their opportunity when the tiger departs.

Other birds which snatch morsels from tiger kills are tree-pies, a long-

Langur monkeys (above) may fall prey to tigers if they leave the safety of the trees. But tigers may be seriously injured by the sharp quills if they attack a porcupine (left).

tailed crow related to the magpie, but more colourful. They sit on surrounding bushes while the tiger feeds, taking advantage of any chance to snatch a tidbit.

In the coastal mangrove forests of the Sundarbans in India and Bangladesh, tigers feed not only on the cheetal and wild boar, but on fish and frogs. They also kill the giant monitor lizards, which grow as long as 2.5 m (9 ft). These lizards, second only to the Komodo dragons of Indonesia in size, and reminiscent of dinosaurs, feed on sea turtles and their eggs, thus creating an unusual marine food chain leading to the tiger. In turn, the monitor lizards scavenge tiger kills.

Tigers may prey on pythons. Indian pythons can grow to a length of 6 m (19.7 ft). One reticulated python, a species found in southeast Asia, grew to 8.4 m (28 ft) in a German zoo, and weighed 113.6 kg (250 lb). Pythons live on small mammals, reptiles and birds. They can kill deer and wild boar by crushing them in their coils. The prey is swallowed whole, the jaws unlocking to allow the mouth to encompass the body.

Adult elephants, rhinoceroses, buffalo and gaur (largest of the wild cattle) have little to fear from the tiger because of their size. Tigers prey on their young if given the chance. But the protective parents can be formidable foes.

ABOVE: The great one-horned rhinoceros has nothing to fear from a tiger when full grown. However, its babies can be easy prey. Mothers will fiercely defend their young.

The tiger has been part of the environment of the people in much of Asia since prehistoric times. Along with elephants, rhinoceroses, deer, monkeys, snakes and eagles, tigers were among the vast array of wild animals in the forests which covered most of the area. Humans were a relatively insignificant part of this world, and lived in the shadow of the wild.

The earliest firm evidence of tigers in human culture is on seals from the Indus Valley civilization of Harappa and Mohenjodaro, in what is now Pakistan. This civilization was the contemporary, 5,000 years ago, of the Nile and Mesopotamian cultures. Tigers are among the many animals, wild and domestic, depicted on the seals, which are believed to have marked ownership of property and were worn as amulets. A horned god on one seal is surrounded by a tiger, an elephant, a rhinoceros and a buffalo. Another shows a hero grappling with two tigers, and is reminiscent of a Sumerian seal showing a similar fight between the hero Gilgamesh and two lions.

The Aryans, warlike cattle breeders who entered India from the northwest some 4,000 years ago, brought with them a rich poetic tradition. This tradition was handed down by word of mouth among the priestly caste and forms the basis of Hinduism. Frequent references to tigers occur in the two great epic poems, the *Mahabharata*

ABOVE: Tigers draw a chariot carrying two demons to join battle with Prince Rama. This scene from the Hindu epic, the Ramayana, is in the Temple of the Emerald Buddha in Bangkok.

and the *Ramayana*, where the tiger is a symbol of beauty, power and ferocity. Verses on the killing of tigers by valiant chiefs appear in the early Tamil poetry of southern India.

The tiger became the mount of the terrible female deity, Durga 'the in-accessible'. Durga is the centre of one of India's greatest festivals, the Durga Puja (Worship of Durga), which lasts for nine days during the September-October moon. At that time, Bengalis parade and worship images of Durga as a beautiful yellow woman riding a fierce tiger. Indian truck drivers often have Durga and her tiger painted on their vehicles.

In China, ever since the days when tigers roamed the country, people have interpreted the marking on its fore-head as the pictogram *Wang*, meaning 'king' and honoured it accordingly. In the 60-year cycle of the Chinese calendar, the tiger is one of 12 animals associated with each of the five elements in turn – earth, iron, water, wood and fire – to denote a year. A boy born in the Year of the Tiger, the king of wild animals, is believed to have the power to ward off evil. A girl, however, needs to be matched to an older man to have equal power. Even in present-day China, children have the character *Wang* painted on their foreheads in wine and mercury during the Year of the Tiger to promote vigour and health. They are given tiger-head caps, and shoes embroidered with tiger heads, and sleep on tiger-shaped pillows to make them robust.

Chinese painters emphasize the power of tigers by depicting them in spectacular, craggy mountain scenes.

Durga, the fierce female Hindu deity (above), is often painted on trucks in India. A Tibetan calendar (left) depicts the tiger (at 8 o'clock) as one of the 12 animals representing the cycle of the years.

and the White Tiger'. Here the tiger is the symbol of the Mountain King or Mountain Spirit. Folk paintings depict the spirit as a white-bearded old man with a tiger. Buildings are still sited, by preference, with mountains to east and west. The Blue Dragon is the guardian of the east and the White Tiger of the West. Dragon and tiger paintings were traditionally hung on middle doors of houses to repel evil. Tigers are said to eat only bad people. However, according to Horay Zoza-yong, founder of the Emille Museum in Seoul, there is a belief that by eating the human body and soul together, the tiger obtains a superior spirit. A notch in the ear is said to indicate each person thus consumed. The museum has a folk painting of a tiger with six notches. Although some tigers were thought to survive in North Korea until a few years ago, they are extinct in South Korea. Nevertheless, the tiger was chosen as the symbol of the 1988 Olympic Games in Seoul.

One of the first Europeans known to have seen tigers was Alexander the Great. He hunted them when he invaded Persia and northwestern India in 330 BC. Seleucus I (312–280 BC), whose empire extended as far as the frontiers of India, presented a tiger to the people of Athens. Two centuries later, the Roman Emperor Augustus received several tigers from an Indian embassy. One of them was probably the first to be seen in Rome. It was a tigress, which Pliny tells us was exhibited by Augustus at the dedication of the Theatre of Marcellus in 11 BC. Other Roman writers mention tigers, including Martial, who described

Sculpted and painted tigers appear frequently in Chinese Buddhist art. The God of Hell, Titsang, is shown riding a tiger.

Tibetan lamas also view the tiger as a powerful creature, able to avert evil. They exorcize the death demon by setting up a mud-plaster tiger and placing on its back the figure of a man clad in silk, whose belly has been stuffed with a paper reading 'Go, thou eating devil, having your face turned to the enemy'.

It is unlikely that any tigers survive today in Korea, but the country is still called the 'Land of the Blue Dragon

tigers drawing chariots in the arena when Domitian returned from wars in Persia in AD 93. Emperor Nero saved a particularly gallant tiger from death in the arena. He named her Phoebe and kept her as a pet. The less-sentimental Emperor Heliogabalus had 51 tigers massacred in the arena on the occasion of his marriage.

Many surviving Roman mosaics depict tigers. The 'Great Hunt' mosaic in the Villa Imperiale in Piazza Armerina, Sicily, shows a mounted hunter clasping a tiger cub as he escapes up the gangway of a ship, while the tigress is diverted by seeing

A Bhutanese greeting card (above) for the Year of the Tiger, 1986. The Roman mosaic (left) dates from 300 AD.

A tigress carries her cub (right) on a Chinese silk scroll. Spanish explorers in the Americas encountered a new big cat, the jaguar (below). They called it 'el Tigre' after the Asian tiger.

herself in a mirror thrown down by the hunter. It illustrates a poem by Claudian about the theft of a tiger cub for a Persian king.

During the early Middle Ages, Europe seems to have forgotten about tigers. Marco Polo, travelling to Asia in the thirteenth century, clearly had not heard of them. He described Kublai Khan as having 'many lions, which are larger than the Babylonian lions, have good skins and a handsome colour, being streaked lengthways with white, black and red stripes'. The Great Khan used them for hunting. Marco Polo said they were taken out in cages with a little dog for company. In this context it is interesting to note that, until recently, a dog shared a

cage with a tiger in the Bangkok Zoo and they were said to be inseparable. Indian naturalist Arjan Singh kept a mongrel dog, which dominated his tame tiger and leopards.

The tiger appeared again in Europe in the second half of the fifteenth century. Yolanda, duchess of Savoy, had one in her palace in Turin. Tigers were also kept at the court of Ferrara. They became quite common in menageries.

On a visit to India in 1558, an English merchant, Ralph Fitch, found tigers plentiful. In Burma he reported that at Cossim (modern Bassein), in the Irrawaddy delta, people built houses on stilts 'for feare of the tygers'.

Spanish explorers in central and southern America named the big cat they found there 'el Tigre'. But it turned out to be a different species, now known to the English-speaking world as the jaguar, a name derived from a Brazilian Indian name.

People dwelling in forests have often felt a sense of the mysterious. Belief in forest spirits, good and evil, has been widespread. Not surprisingly, the tiger, mostly an unseen and silent intangible presence that can dramatically erupt on the scene, figures strongly in forest folklore. The Minangkabau people of central Sumatra are Muslims, but they use tiger-capturing songs called *dendang marindu harimau* (*harimau* means tiger) that originated before the advent of Islam. They consider most tigers as 'good' if they stay in

BELOW: Using a series of paintings, a folk singer teaches people how to live alongside tigers in the Indian Sundarbans.

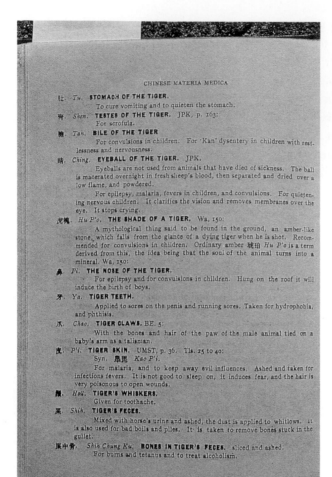

CHINESE MATERIA MEDICA

肚. *Tu.* **STOMACH OF THE TIGER.**
 To cure vomiting and to quieten the stomach.

肾. *Shen.* **TESTES OF THE TIGER.** JPK, p. 163:
 For scrofula.

膽. *Tan.* **BILE OF THE TIGER**
 For convulsions in children. For 'Kan' dysentery in children with restlessness and nervousness.

睛. *Ching.* **EYEBALL OF THE TIGER.** JPK.
 Eyeballs are not used from animals that have died of sickness. The ball is macerated overnight in fresh sheep's blood, then separated and dried over a low flame, and powdered.
 For epilepsy, malaria, fevers in children, and convulsions. For quietening nervous children. It clarifies the vision and removes membranes over the eye. It stops crying.

虎魄. *Hu P'o.* **THE SHADE OF A TIGER.** Wa, 150:
 A mythological thing said to be found in the ground, an amber-like stone, which falls from the glance of a dying tiger when he is shot. Recommended for convulsions in children. Ordinary amber 琥珀 *Hu P'o* is a term derived from this, the idea being that the soul of the animal turns into a mineral. Wa, 150:

鼻. *Pi.* **THE NOSE OF THE TIGER.**
 For epilepsy and for convulsions in children. Hung on the roof it will induce the birth of boys.

牙. *Ya.* **TIGER TEETH.**
 Applied to sores on the penis and running sores. Taken for hydrophobia, and phthisis.

爪. *Chao.* **TIGER CLAWS.** BE. 5:
 With the bones and hair of the paw of the male animal tied on a baby's arm as a talisman.

皮. *P'i.* **TIGER SKIN.** UMST, p. 36. Tls. 25 to 40:
 Syn. 黑皮 *Kao P'i.*
 For malaria, and to keep away evil influences. Ashed and taken for infections fevers. It is not good to sleep on, it induces fear, and the hair is very poisonous to open wounds.

鬚. *Hsü.* **TIGER'S WHISKERS.**
 Given for toothache.

屎. *Shih.* **TIGER'S FECES.**
 Mixed with horse's urine and ashed, the dust is applied to whitlows. It is also used for bad boils and piles. It is taken to remove bones stuck in the gullet.

屎中骨. *Shih Chung Ku.* **BONES IN TIGER'S FECES.** sliced and ashed.
 For burns and tetanus and to treat alcoholism.

Chinese use animal parts extensively for medicine. The Chinese pharmacopaeia (right), prepared in 1597 by Li Shih-Chen, is still used. A 19th century drawing (below) shows a fierce Royal Bengal Tiger.

their own land. But some stray into human territory and commit sins by killing people. Then villagers call in a shaman – a man who communicates with the spirit world using his magical powers. Most powerful are the tiger-catcher shamans. They place a cage in the forest, baited with a goat. Sitting nearby in the darkness they play a long bamboo flute and softly sing melodies handed down from father to son for countless generations. The songs politely call on the tiger to enter the cage. It may take many nights before the tiger comes. When it enters the shamans close the door. They claim that even if they are not present they know when a tiger has entered and can go and trap it. The tiger is then speared to death.

Were-tigers are a widely accepted phenomenon among forest people in southern Asia, playing the same role as were-wolves in European folklore. Stories tell of men and women who transform themselves into tigers. Lieutenant-Colonel A. Locke, who hunted tigers in peninsular Malaysia, recounted how a stranger, already looked upon with suspicion by villagers following an outbreak of killing of livestock and people, was killed when he sheltered in a tiger cage baited with a goat. His explanation that he was hiding from a tiger was not accepted. His double life as a tiger had been proved to the villagers' satisfaction.

Many people in tiger areas never refer to the big cat directly, preferring a nickname such as 'Mr Stripes' or 'Our Forest Friend'.

Springing from belief in the power of the tiger comes acceptance that

parts of its body make good medicine. Bones are prized to cure ulcers, rheumatism, fevers and burns, and to drive away evil influences. Flesh is a stomach tonic. Blood builds the constitution and strengthens willpower. The nose, hung on the roof, will induce the birth of boys. These strongly held beliefs have brought tigers to the verge of extinction in China, and demand has led to the poaching of other species, such as leopards and golden cats, as substitutes.

The reputation of the tiger has fared badly compared with that of the lion. The *Compleat Universal Display of Animated Nature*, published in 1785, declared: 'There is a sort of cruelty in the devastations of this creature, unknown to the generous lion; as well as a kind of cowardice in its sudden retreat on any disappointment.' During the same period the poet William Blake clearly viewed its 'fearful symmetry' with awe. 'Did he who made the Lamb make thee?' he asked.

ABOVE: Henri Rousseau never saw a tiger in the wild, but his painting, now in the National Gallery in London, captures the atmosphere of the jungle.

ABOVE: 'Would you like to sin with Elinor Glyn on a tiger skin.' The famous jingle obviously inspired this poster.

minds of many people. Even so, that implacable hunter of man-eaters, Jim Corbett, insisted that the tiger was 'a large-hearted gentleman'. He recalled his childhood wandering in jungles full of tigers, sleeping on the ground by a small fire, and standing calmly to allow a tiger to pass on its way.

In 1964, American biologist George Schaller began pioneer studies in Kanha National Park in central India. On foot among the tigers, he swept away their image as ever-bloodthirsty jungle tyrants with illuminating reports on their social and family life.

At that time tigers were still heavily hunted. But, by the mid-1970s, as alarm at their rarity spread, tigers had gained at least legal protection throughout most of their range. In India and Nepal, intensive conservation had begun. Within a few years, tigers in some well-managed areas lost their fear of people. Not only scientific researchers, but occasional visitors too, have been able to watch them hunting, playing and relaxing, often looking like everyone's pet cat. Needless to say, unlike Schaller, they do not go on foot among tigers, but stay secure on the backs of elephants or in jeeps.

The tiger remains a formidable figure, but still, in some places, the local tiger, who takes an occasional cow but otherwise does no harm, is looked upon affectionately. Some men on bicycles met a tiger strolling down a road in northern India recently. They dismounted and stood quietly by the roadside as the tiger passed. Asked afterwards if they were not frightened, they replied: 'No, sahib, that tiger was deep in thought'.

British hunters boasted of their triumphs over raging tigers, and their narrow escapes from death during the hunt. Some were also good naturalists and left valuable records in books and in the *Journal of the Bombay Natural History Society*. But a moving account of 'two beautiful animals' playing together ends with the words: 'The male was then shot.' The abundance of tigers until this century appears to have absolved the hunters from any feeling of guilt at killing them.

From the grim deeds of hunters' tales, the words 'tiger' and 'man-eater' became virtually synonymous in the

SIX

MAN-
EATERS

Fishermen and
woodcutters get
taken by man-eating
tigers in the
Sundarbans. The
tigers even swim out
to boats like this one
(above) to take
human prey.
A woodcutter (above
right) demonstrates
how a tiger seized
his friend by the
neck while they
were eating
breakfast.

Hair-raising tales told by hunters over the centuries have projected a misleading image of the tiger as a relentless killer and man-eater. An eighteenth-century encyclopaedia declared: 'Tigers are one of the most terrible scourges of the countries they inhabit . . . Fortunately for mankind, this animal is not very common.'

Another old book on India said boat crews on the River Ganges were provided with hatchets to chop off the paws of any tigers that tried to climb aboard. Jim Corbett wrote: 'There is no more terrible thing than to live and have one's being under the shadow of a man-eater'. Trailing the Champawat man-eater, which had killed 434 people before he shot it, Corbett found the inhabitants of one village in a state of abject fear behind locked doors. No one had emerged for five days.

In 1792, an Englishman was taken by a tiger in broad daylight while sitting with friends on an island in the Ganges delta. Ironically, he was the son of Sir Hector Munro, who had gained fame for his victory over Tippu Sultan, the so-called 'Tiger of Mysore'. Tippu Sultan so hated the English that he kept a mechanical model (now in a London museum) of a tiger eating an Englishman to the accompaniment of realistic groans.

ABOVE: The broken
teeth of a stuffed
man-eater shows its
bad condition and
inability to catch
normal prey.

India was not the only country to report man-eaters. In Siberia, during the early years of this century, Cossack troops were despatched to kill tigers which were raiding the camps of Chinese construction workers on the Trans-Baikal Railway. American hunter Harry Caldwell said that the legendary 'blue tigers' in China's Fujian Province, were man-eaters. One had killed 60 people in a few weeks.

Today, the incidence of tigers killing people is very low. The only long-standing exception is in the mangrove jungles of the Sundarbans, where the great rivers Ganges and Brahmaputra flow into the Bay of Bengal, south of Calcutta. Here attacks on humans are widespread and endemic. A French traveller in India in the seventeenth century, François Bernier, described Sundarbans tigers swimming out to boats to take fishermen. Similar incidents occur today. Honey-collectors and wood-cutters, as well as fishermen, are killed in these forests. In the Indian sector of the Sundarbans alone, 521 deaths by tigers were officially recorded between 1975 and mid-1989. At least as many have been killed in the contiguous forests in Bangladesh.

The Sundarbans tigers are reputed to be able to board a boat noiselessly, scarcely even rocking it. A typical

A Nepalese school teacher (below) was killed when he surprised a tiger on a river bank. Tigers have also become a problem in the Soviet Far East (bottom).

incident took place in May 1969. Nagar Ali, a fisherman, was cooking supper on his boat one night when he heard a splash. Looking around, he found that his companion, Malek Molla, to whom he had been talking, had disappeared. Nagar Ali flashed his torch over the water. Its beam fell on a tiger standing on the bank, holding Malek Molla's body in its jaws, like a cat with a fish. It moved into the jungle. The half-eaten body was found next morning.

The problem of killer tigers in the Sundarbans is unique. Only one other serious outbreak has occurred recently in India. In Kheri District, near the Nepalese frontier, nearly 200 people have been killed by tigers in the past 10 years. Eight tigers have been shot, including five confirmed man-eaters.

Tigers are not man-eaters by nature. Most tigers avoid people, and it is a curious fact that they do not regard them as prey. A tiger taken by surprise may make a pre-emptive attack and kill. So may a tigress defending her

cubs from an intruder. But it is then unusual for the tiger to eat the body. Such casual confrontations account for most tiger killings, outside the Sundarbans.

In November 1979, a tiger came up a river bank in Nepal at dawn. It came face to face with schoolteacher Trilochan Paudel on his way for a morning bathe. The tiger leapt on Trilochan. Its long canine teeth stabbed into his skull, killing him instantly. Trilochan's fellow villagers shouted the alarm. The tiger ran off, leaving him lying on the stubble field, blood oozing from his crushed head. The tiger was trapped and tranquillized next day and removed to Kathmandu zoo. It was not a man-eater. It is unlikely it would have become one.

A similar incident occurred in 1985 in the Corbett National Park in India. An English ornithologist, David Hunt, left his group to pursue a bird into dense jungle. When he failed to re-appear, his companions followed and found a tiger sitting by his body. It

Hungry man-eaters stalk the streets in Soviet Far East

From Christopher Walker
Nakhodka, Soviet Far East

Last Thursday, Mr Gennady Kiseliev, a Red Army soldier on leave at his surburban home near this modern, bustling Soviet port, drew back the bedroom curtains and found himself face to face through the frosted window with a man-eating Amur tiger, which had strayed far from the frozen forests in search of food.

It was the latest example of a disturbing natural phenomenon which is causing increasing concern to the Soviet authorities, who have now introduced an emergency programme to deal with the little-publicized fact that, for the first time in 100 years, wild tigers have once again begun prowling the streets of the main built-up areas in the Soviet Far East.

In an attempt to prevent panic among urban dwellers in this remote, mineral-rich region, the development of which is crucial to

Mr Gorbachov's drive to rescue the Soviet economy, a special television programme was recently broadcast, in which three professional hunters sought to reassure the population about the measures being taken to cope with the tiger menace.

Only a few days before Mr Kiseliev's unnerving confrontation, workers at the main container terminal at Nakhodka, on the Sea of Japan, failed to arrive for the morning shift because their commuter train was held up by a large Amur tiger — specimens of which can reach more than 10 ft in length — sitting on the tracks.

Mr Constantin Kovolchok, the unflappable-looking captain of a large Soviet container vessel which sails regularly from the port to Australia, explained: "I can imagine how they felt. I was recently approached by one of the creatures when I was driving my car home. It was very frightening. At first I thought it was a stray cow, until it got up close."

In recognition of the dangers now posed to both livestock and humans (last year a tiger was shot near a crowded trolley-bus stop on the outskirts of the main Far-Eastern city, Vladivostok), a new division has been created in the Russian Republic's hunting directorate to supervise control of the predators, using a number of measures, including helicopters.

A three-year ban has been imposed on the hunting of smaller animals, such as wild boar and deer, which provided the magnificent-looking wild cats with their main source of food.

Widespread poaching of these animals by hunters with increasingly sophisticated weapons, together with the rapid development of the sprawling wilds of eastern Siberia, where the wind-chill factor can push temperatures below −100 C, are two of the reasons why the starving tigers are being forced to prey close to human settlements.

On one night last year, a tiger

killed 11 pigs on a farm in the Primorsky region, and a number of attacks on humans have been reported in the press.

A third reason is the growth in the population of the Amur tiger, an endangered species which has recovered from the critical period just before the Second World War, when its numbers dwindled to 30. The latest official total puts it at 300, with each male jealously protecting an area of some 115 square miles as an exclusive hunting zone.

"Although these tigers are marvellous animals, they are now a real threat to life, and we have to take urgent action to deal with them before the problem gets worse," said Mr Viktor Gnysdilov, Deputy Mayor of Nakhodka, a city of concrete apartment buildings with a population of 178,000.

Despite the outlawing of tiger-hunting here 40 years ago, and the imposition of stiff 10,000 rouble (£10,000) fines for breaching the

ban, Mr Gnysdilov said that a new count was now being organized, after which further permits for killing all the Amur tigers which could not be supported by the surrounding forest would be issued by the Government. More than 20 such permits were issued last year.

Distinguished both by its size and by the unique spread of its paws, the pads of which are often more than four inches wide, the Amur tiger is the official symbol of Vladivostok, the headquarters of the Soviet Pacific fleet.

But with tiger sightings now becoming a regular occurrence, and attacks growing more frequent, even the Soviet protectionists we met here appeared to accept that urgent action would have to be taken.

After the shooting of beasts above the optimum number, one suggestion is for the creation of a protection zone for tigers and hoofed animals within existing game reserves, followed by the opening of new reserves.

had eaten part of his leg before the body was recovered. The authorities immediately ordered the tiger to be shot for fear of further incidents in this popular wildlife tourist area. But it was reprieved when it became clear that it had not been stalking the ornithologist. He had stumbled on it when he entered the dense cover where it was resting.

In Thailand's Khao Yai National Park in 1984 there was a different type of incident. A young schoolgirl, Srinival Interadechia, daughter of a forest guard, dropped her pencil through the verandah floorboards of her home. The house was on stilts, so she crawled underneath to retrieve it. Suddenly, she was grabbed by a tiger. She screamed as the tiger carried her off in its jaws. Park guards rushed out shouting. The tiger dropped her and retreated. Srinival died on the way to hospital.

That night the tiger came back again, reached up at a window where a guard was leaning on the sill inside, and killed him with one blow of its forepaw. The third night it appeared again, and this time it was shot dead.

ABOVE: Mangroves are rich prawn areas. Fishermen are willing to risk death from man-eating tigers in the Sundarbans, on the shore of the Bay of Bengal.

Wild honey from the Indian Sundarbans (above) is a great delicacy. But the price often includes the lives of collectors at risk from man-eaters. Guard Booncherd Leksat (right) shot a tiger which killed a young girl in Khao Yai National Park, Thailand.

This tiger could easily have become a man-eater. There was no record of it having attacked a human before, and it might have mistaken the girl for a dog when she crawled under the house. But it was found to be old, with worn and broken teeth. It was probably desperate for food and had been seen in the area for two or three weeks before the attack.

Although tigers mainly take live prey, they sometimes eat carrion. Corbett speculated that, in his day, some had got a taste for human flesh from the bodies of victims of the 1918 influenza epidemic in northern India. Deaths in some hill villages were so numerous that relatives could not afford to burn the dead. The bodies were thrown into ravines, where tigers scavenged them. Those tigers may have developed a taste for the flesh and become man-killers when they realized that people were easy targets.

A Vietnam veteran, Major A.D. Ackels, said pilots and grave registration squads saw tigers scavenging bodies on battlefields. In one incident, a tiger grabbed a marine by the knee as he lay in his foxhole behind a barbed wire fence near Da Nang. When it tried to drag him away, he became entangled in the wire. The tiger tugged to free him, while he shouted for help. It ran off when his comrades arrived, leaving him with a mangled knee – and a most unusual war story.

Tiger attacks on people have been reported in recent years from Sumatra, particularly in areas where people from the over-populated islands of Java, Bali and Madura are being settled in newly cleared forest areas.

In the USSR there has been concern about the increasing number of confrontations between people and tigers in the eastern maritime territory of Primorje, north of Vladivostok, although no deaths have been reported. A tiger was even shot in the suburbs of Vladivostok city. The newspaper *Trud* reported that 20 permits were issued in 1985 to kill tigers wandering near populated areas.

The Indian government insists that the circumstances of any attack should be investigated. If an attack has clearly been accidental, the tiger is given the benefit of the doubt but kept under observation. Any tiger that is obviously hunting humans is shot, or tranquillized and removed to a zoo.

The killer tigers of Kheri graphically illustrate a modern problem. The encroachment of human activity on wild areas has confined wildlife to a few 'islands' in an ocean of humanity. Kheri was once prime wildlife habitat with few people. But over the past 30 years it has been converted to rich farmland, noted for sugar cane, which is grown right up to the boundaries of the Dudhwa National Park. For a tiger, sugar cane is like long grass. Tigresses find it an ideal haven for giving birth to their cubs. Deer and pig outside the park have been almost wiped out by poachers, so tigers have a hard task in finding prey. In the cane-fields, people sometimes come face to face with tigers and are killed.

Tigers living on the edge of the park, where deer and pig are less common, also find livestock easy prey. This, again, brings them into close contact with people and increases the possibility

ABOVE: Hindus and Muslims share a shrine in the Sundarbans to pray for protection from man-eating tigers.

of accidental killings. It is in these circumstances that a few tigers, especially tigresses under the stress of finding food for their young, have turned to human prey. There is then a danger that a tigress may teach her cubs to hunt people.

The Sundarbans Forests pose a different problem. This area of 8,000 km² (3,000 sq. miles) of mangrove forests, tidal creeks and rivers in India and Bangladesh contains between 500

and 600 tigers – the largest single population to survive anywhere in the world. Dr Hubert Hendrichs, a German biologist, carried out a study in 1971. He suggested that the tigers' ferocity might be linked to drinking salt water because of the lack of fresh-water sources. Nevertheless, he estimated that, even here, fewer than one per cent of the tigers were dedicated man-eaters, although perhaps one-third would attack humans on sight and

might eat them. The remainder avoided humans and would only attack in self-defence if suddenly confronted.

The Indian Sundarbans is now almost entirely reserved for tigers. There are no settlements. But despite the dangers, men and women still go into the reserve – with or without official permission – to catch fish and prawns, and to collect wood and gather honey in the dense jungles. The wildlife authorities give them fire-crackers to scare tigers. But their faith still rests mainly in the jungle gods.

Hindus and Muslims, often antagonistic elsewhere, pray for protection at joint shrines before images of Banbibi, the Hindu goddess of the forest, and Shah Jungli, the Muslim king of the jungle. They place mangrove leaves, sweetmeats and small coins at the feet of the images, and pray: 'In the name of Banbibi, say Allah, Allah. And in the name of

ABOVE: A tiger would get a sharp shock if it attacked this dummy woodsman. It has been wired to a battery. It is hoped that tigers will thus learn not to attack people.

Dhakin Roy, say Bhagwan.' This prayer links the Hindu goddess, Banbibi, with the Muslim name for God, Allah, and the Hindu equivalent, Bhagwan. Dhakin Roy is a nickname for the tiger, for the local people never refer to the great cat by name, for fear of attracting attention.

Until 1971, bounties were still paid for shooting tigers in the Sundarbans, but since then they have been completely protected. It is now a question of protecting people who enter the reserve to earn their living. Experiments are being tried with modern technology. Dummies are dressed in used clothing, which is drenched in urine to provide a genuine human

scent. The dummies are primed with electric wires linked to batteries. The tiger gets a shock, but a fuse immediately blows, eliminating the danger of electrocution. Several tigers have suffered shocks. Scratch marks on the boat of a dummy fisherman showed where one had recoiled. The back and loincloth of an electrified dummy woodcutter in the depth of the forest was ripped by another tiger. In this way, the authorities hope to teach tigers that humans are dangerous.

Fresh-water ponds have been dug, so that tigers are not dependent on saline water from the creeks. Pigs have also been bred for release just inside the reserve to ensure that tigers remain

ABOVE: A tiger, perhaps the local man-eater, comes to drink in the late evening in the Sundarbans. Fresh water is provided in case tigers may become aggressive from drinking saline water in this delta area.

MAN-EATERS

ABOVE: A peacock butterfly has large eye-like spots on its wings to deter predatory birds. This notion has been copied for the face-masks designed to fool tigers.

well fed and are not tempted to prey on livestock, and possibly people, in villages along the perimeter.

The most promising solution has been the introduction of a two-faced approach to trick tigers into abandoning their human prey. Since tigers normally attack from behind, rather than face-to-face, cheap plastic masks have been distributed to forest workers to wear on the back of the head. The result has been dramatic. In 1987 thousands of workers began taking the masks with them when they went to fish, cut wood

or collect honey. In two and a half years only one man wearing a mask has been killed by a tiger, and he was attacked from the side on the lower half of the body. Tigers have been seen stalking workers, but failing to attack.

Local people warn that tigers are too clever to be deceived for long. But many animals, such as butterflies and caterpillars, have evolved large eye-like spots on their backs, which deter predatory birds. As yet, there is no sign that the birds have become wise to the trick.

THE
DECLINE
OF THE
TIGER

A century ago forests still covered most of southern Asia. The human population was only one third of what it is today – about 900 million compared with an estimated 2,715 million in mid-1989. There were no mechanical vehicles, and so human mobility was limited. Malaria made many places unsuitable for human settlement. Wild animals reigned supreme in the forests. They were hunted and trapped in the vicinity of settled areas, but elsewhere were virtually undisturbed by people.

Tigers were very common. One can only guess at what their numbers might have been. British naturalist E.P. Gee estimated that there might have been 40,000 tigers in the Indian subcontinent in the early twentieth century. Perhaps a similar number ranged through southeast Asia, China and eastern Siberia.

The number of tigers recorded as killed in official documents and hunters' journals provides an indication of how prolific they were. Kailash Sankhala, a leading Indian tiger specialist, carried out widespread research. He found that in one district in what is now Maharashtra State in India, villagers killed as many as 1,053 tigers between 1821 and 1828. A single British officer, Colonel William Rice, shot 93 in central India between 1850 and 1854. George Udney Yule bagged 400 during 25 years in the Bengal Civil Service. In the princedom of Cooch Behar in northeast India, 295 tigers were shot in the 27 years between 1880 and 1907. One Gordon Cumming shot 173 tigers in the year 1863/4. In the Himalayan district of Kumaon, rewards were paid for killing 624 tigers (and 2,718 leopards) between 1860 and 1880. Where tigers were a nuisance they were officially destroyed. Thus, one official, a Captain Caulfield, poisoned 93 tigers in 1874. Despite this slaughter there was no apparent reduction in the tiger population. With plenty of prey and large, undisturbed areas in the forests, tigers were able to breed freely and successfully. A territory was immediately re-occupied by another tiger when the resident tiger was shot.

The slaughter continued in the first half of the twentieth century. When King George V went hunting with the maharajah of Nepal in 1911, the party shot 39 tigers in 11 days. As late as the winter of 1938/9, when the British viceroy, Lord Linlithgow, was the maharajah's guest of honour, 120 tigers and 27 leopards were shot in 10 weeks. Across the border, in India, the tiger bag for 1938 was 891. Many Indian princes claimed 'scores' of over 100. The raja of Gauripur shot 500 in his lifetime; the maharajah of Gwalior 700. The record goes to the maharajah of Surguja, who, by 1964, claimed to have shot 1,150 tigers. Palaces and hunting lodges were carpeted with tiger skins, and the heads arrayed on the walls.

A favoured hunting technique was to put out a young buffalo or goat as bait overnight, or to sit on a tree platform over a kill to await the tiger's return. This meant sitting quietly so as not to alert the tiger and deter it from coming. On a moonlit night the tiger could be seen. But when it was dark, the hunter listened for the sound of bones being crunched. He then

switched on the torch lashed to the barrel of his rifle, hopefully illuminating the tiger, and fired. Often the tiger was not shot dead, but disappeared into the jungle. The hunter then had to follow the blood trail when day came, hoping to find the tiger dead, but ready to shoot if it was alive. Some forgot to take precautions. A tomb in central India bears the epitaph of one Lewis Gordon 'killed while following up a wounded tiger with a gun he had forgotten to load'. Many cemeteries include graves with the words 'died of injuries received from a tiger'.

The grand style of hunting was to go out on elephants seated in a box-like howdah. The tiger would be driven to the hunter by lines of local men hired as beaters, or by assistants on elephants. In Nepal, several dozen elephants were used to surround the tiger. As it attempted to escape the hunters fired, the guest of honour being allowed the

RIGHT: Large wild animals are now confined to reserves in much of Asia. This river marks the boundary between Nepal's Chitwan National Park with its thick forest, and former tiger habitat which has been converted to agriculture.

first shot. Many times the tiger, in its rage, would leap on to an elephant. Well-trained elephants stood up to the powerful assault, shaking the tiger off. A cool hunter could shoot the tiger as it clung to the elephant's head. But an inexperienced or poorly trained elephant might run in terror while the hunters tried desperately to cling on – not always successfully. A further refinement of this style of hunting was to set out a cloth barrier around the cover in which the tiger was hidden.

World War II marked a watershed. War technology produced the jeep, which could go almost anywhere over rough country. The deep forests were no longer sanctuaries for wildlife. Hunting rifles benefited from research into more efficient weaponry, and guns were more easily available. There was massive cutting of forests for building materials for the war effort.

Tiger expert Jim Corbett was already alarmed at the decrease in wildlife. He warned the British viceroy, Lord Wavell, in 1946, that only 3,000 to 4,000 tigers were left. He predicted that they would be practically extinct in 10 to 15 years.

In 1947, India and Pakistan became independent nations as the British left. The princes, whose territories covered two-fifths of India, lost their autocratic rule. People overwhelmed their hunting estates. A massive slaughter of wildlife ensued. Tigers were killed, but, equally important, their prey was wiped out.

THE DECLINE OF
THE TIGER

Cubs starved to death. Hunting controls collapsed. Crop protection guns were freely available and were used to kill any wild animal. Poaching was rife. Hunters roamed the forests at night in jeeps equipped with powerful spotlights discarded from wartime Dakota aircraft. They shot at any reflected eyes. In some famous tiger hunting reserves, almost no large mammals were left.

Equalling the jeep in opening up the wild country was the advent of the pesticide, DDT. Malarial areas could now be cleared and converted to settlement and agriculture. The great belt of forest, grasslands and swamps along the foot of the Himalayas known as the *terai*, where the maharajahs of Nepal had conducted their great hunts for tigers, elephants, rhinoceroses and buffalo, was transformed during the 1950s and 1960s as hillmen descended in Nepal to farm the rich land. Large-scale agricultural development began on the Indian side of the border. Only a small fraction of the terai wilderness survives.

Foreign hunters headed for India and Nepal to obtain the supreme trophy. A huge trade in tiger skins developed. Villagers, already annoyed by tigers killing their cattle, put pesticides into the carcasses to poison them. Whole tiger families died. The furs could bring in a year's normal income for the farmer.

In 1955 Corbett, who had by then migrated to Kenya, wrote to *The Times* of London suggesting that only 2,000 tigers survived. His estimate was not based on a specific census. But nor were others. Counting secretive animals in forest is well-nigh impossible. All estimates were compilations of the impressions of local forest staff.

However, Corbett's figures were close to those produced by J.C. Daniel, curator of the Bombay Natural History Society, and Kailash Sankhala, a member of the Indian Forest Service, who received a Nehru Fellowship for his work. They put the figure in 1969 at about 2,500, and fast declining. It was at this stage that a worried international community stepped in. In 1969, the International Union for Conservation of Nature and Natural Resources (IUCN) met in Delhi and called for urgent action to save the tiger from extinction. This set in motion a whole range of conservation measures.

In China, massive destruction of tiger habitat had occurred following removal of protective laws on forests by the Qing dynasty in 1870. When Mao Tse Tung proclaimed the victory of the Communist armies in China in 1949, bringing an end to decades of turmoil in this vast country, people began to spread through the heart of the tiger's habitat. Bounties were paid for killing tigers. Thousands died. The Siberian or Manchurian tiger, renamed in China as the Northeast China tiger, was finally given protection in 1962. It was even declared a 'rare and precious species'. Nevertheless, illegal hunting continued and numbers estimated at 150 in the mid-1970s are now reduced to only about 30, all confined to a small region close to the Soviet border. A few tigers were reported in North Korea in the 1970s, but there has been no recent news of any.

LEFT: The eyes of sambar deer shine in a spotlight, making it easy for poachers to take aim.

ABOVE: Twice as many Siberian tigers live in zoos now as in the wild. Their last sanctuary is in the Soviet Far East. There are a few in China.

In the USSR, the Siberian tiger once ranged from Lake Baikal to the Sea of Okhotsk. Spread of human settlement, combined with heavy hunting, gradually reduced the range. In 1940, the first census in the USSR put the number at 20 to 30, confined to areas north of Vladivostok. Hunting was banned in 1947, since when tiger numbers have increased strongly. The lowest estimate by Russian biologists is now about 200 tigers, while the highest is about 350.

The South China tiger is vanishing for a variety of reasons. It used to live in the richest agricultural areas of the heartland of China. Despite its role at the centre of Chinese religion and culture, and the fact that it is a sub-species found nowhere else in the world, the Communists declared it a pest, along with sparrows and rats. It was hunted mercilessly by armed units and peasants. Fur trade was officially encouraged. According to Chinese scientists Lu Houji and Sheng Helin, about 3,000 were killed in 30 years before hunting was banned in 1977. By then the population numbered only hundreds. Today, Lu Houji puts it at less than 50. The value of tiger bones and other parts for medicine ensure that poachers give the tiger no respite.

During the 1930s tigers from China visited Hong Kong's New Territories on the mainland. They even swam across to the island, where the last known was shot in 1942 by the Japanese.

In peninsular Malaysia, the area occupied by humans early in this century was described as 'infinitesimal compared with the extent of the forest'. But some of the finest tropical timbers in the world grow in the lowland forests of Malaysia. They were much in demand for furniture, flooring and construction. Exploitation accelerated after independence in 1957. Malaysia became one of the world's principal timber exporters. Vast areas have also been converted to oil palm plantations. Now, less than half the country is covered by forest. Lieutenant-Colonel A. Locke put the number of tigers at nearly 3,000 in 1950. But, with the loss of habitat, the tiger population has dropped to about 600.

Thailand, too, has experienced massive clearance of the forests which once blanketed the country. From being a timber exporter, Thailand actually became an importer of tropical timber. In 1977, the tiger population was thought to be about 500, a figure that may still be correct.

The island of Java, site of Indonesia's capital, Bandung, has always been densely populated because of the great

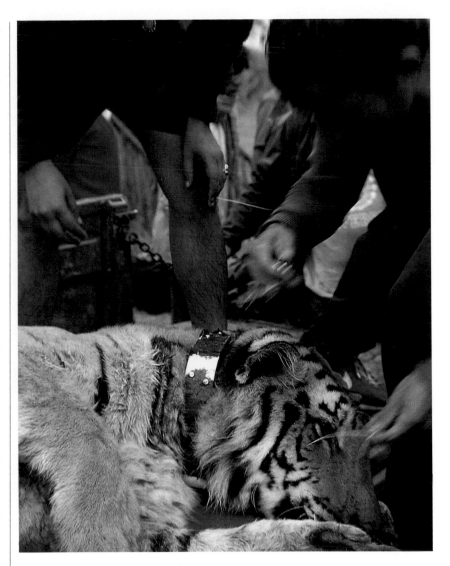

fertility of its volcanic soils. By the end of the war, few tigers were left, mainly in the extreme west and the extreme east. The last records were of three tigers in the eastern reserve of Meru Betiri in 1980, since when there have been no authenticated reports. On the equally densely populated island of Bali, east of Java, the tiger has not been seen since the 1940s. In Bali and Java the tiger must be presumed extinct.

Sumatra, on the other hand, had a relatively low human population and

ABOVE. Tiger whiskers are considered potent medicine in some Asian countries. This tiger lost his while he was tranquillized.

THE TIGER WHICH WAS SHOT AT FANLING IN 1915 BY SUPT. OF POLICE MR. BURLINGHAM
AFTER IT HAD KILLED TWO POLICE OFFICERS WHO WERE SEARCHING FOR IT.

一九一五年白靈威警司於新界粉嶺射枝此虎 事前曾有警官兩名在搜
獵該老虎時遇害

ABOVE: Tigers used to be found on the mainland near Hong Kong, but were intensively hunted. They even swam to the island, where the last was shot in 1942.

was covered with forests in which tigers were common. But, as elsewhere in southeast Asia, the forests have been heavily exploited to export timber for foreign exchange. In the past few years, wild areas have been transformed as the Indonesian government settled several million people in Sumatra from the overcrowded islands of Java, Madura and Bali. The settlers' livestock has been attacked by tigers, and some people have been killed. Despite legal protection, tigers have been poisoned and even openly hunted by officials. Smuggling of skins to *entrepôts*, such as Singapore, is easy. The remaining tiger population may now number anything from a few hundred to more than a thousand.

By the end of the 1960s the Caspian tiger had gone from the USSR. Increasing human settlement, economic development and intensive hunting are the reasons given by Soviet specialists. In Iran, the last-known Caspian tiger was shot in 1959. Loss of habitat to agriculture and hunting had already reduced its numbers to a minimum. Some fresh skins appeared in eastern Turkey in 1972, but since then there has been no evidence that the Caspian tiger survives.

When wildlife experts from all over the world gathered in Delhi in 1969 for the General Assembly of the International Union for Conservation of Nature and Natural Resources (IUCN), the threat of early extinction of the tiger dominated the meeting.

Kailash Sankhala, a member of the Indian Forest Service fresh from a two-year study of the tiger, shook the assembly with his estimate that the number of tigers in India had been reduced to 2,500. Skins had been freely exported, and, even after a ban was imposed in 1986, 2,345 tiger and leopard skins went out in the following six months. That did not include those taken by tourists and other foreigners. Five hundred tiger skins were said to be in shops in Delhi alone.

The assembly called for an immediate moratorium on tiger hunting and for scientific studies to establish how many tigers existed and what their prospects were, wherever in the world they occurred. At the same time, the Bengal tiger was declared 'endangered' and joined all seven other subspecies in the IUCN's authoritative *Red Data Book of Endangered Species.*

Despite opposition from hunters and hunting organizations, as well as from foresters, who thought that stricter control of hunting would suffice to save the animal, tiger hunt-

ing was completely banned in all the states of India by mid-1971. Other tiger countries followed suit, except for Burma, which still has no laws to protect its tigers. By official decree, the tiger replaced the lion as India's national animal, although the lion still remains India's crest.

Meanwhile, an all-India census in 1972 produced a shock total of only 1,800 surviving tigers. Guy Mountfort, a British naturalist and trustee of the World Wildlife Fund (WWF), announced a million-dollar appeal to save the tiger, under the banner Operation Tiger. Mountfort flew to Dehli and promised Prime Minister Indira Gandhi aid for tiger conservation. She

immediately established a task force to prepare a comprehensive programme. Eight special tiger reserves were established. On 1 April, 1973, the Indian government launched Project Tiger, and Mrs Gandhi herself took the chair of the steering committee.

Project Tiger took an ecological approach, recognizing that protection from hunting alone would not save the tiger. It was essential to rehabilitate and conserve the whole living web of plants and animals over extensive areas. Poaching of tigers and of their prey animals, especially deer, had to be reduced to a minimum. Cattle and goats sent to graze in reserves by local villages had to be excluded because they were

ABOVE: Kailash Sankhala (right) was the first director of India's Project Tiger, one of the most successful wildlife conservation programmes.

THIS IS OUR TERRITORY. DON'T DISTURB. WE ARE HERE TO KEEP THE NATURAL BALANCE.

বিনা অনুমতিতে প্রকল্প এলাকায় ঢুকবেন না ·P/D. S.T.R.

destroying the vegetation. There were even villages inside reserves.

Mrs Gandhi put Project Tiger under the charge of a senior cabinet minister, Dr Karan Singh. Kailash Sankhala was appointed director. The first task was to persuade the state governments to forego the considerable revenue earned from logging in the new tiger reserves. The central government's offer of compensation overcame the problem.

Meanwhile, WWF raised funds in Europe and North America for the purchase of equipment. It provided jeeps, motorcycles, bicycles, night vision scopes and cameras for guards and research work. Radio networks were established in the reserves to

A notice (above) warns visitors to the Sundarbans Tiger Reserve, near Calcutta, that they are entering the tiger's domain, and should respect it. Reserve Director Pranabes Sanyal (right) patrols the mangrove delta in a jet boat provided by WWF.

facilitate control of poaching and, equally important, of the fires which ravaged large areas during the hot, dry season.

Under the keen eye of Indira Gandhi, Project Tiger made strong progress in India. In 1975, a party of 28 European children were invited to India by the government as a reward for raising funds. They had the excitement of seeing tigers in the wild.

Hopes for the tiger in India increased with a census in 1979, which indicated that numbers had risen to 3,000. Improved census methods and wider coverage accounted for a considerable part of the 66 per cent increase over the 1972 census, but it was clear that conservation efforts were succeeding.

Subsequent censuses counted growing tiger numbers, reaching more than 4,000 in 1989. The number of special reserves for tigers was increased to 17.

Project Tiger was, at the same time, helping to check the rapid decline of all Indian wildlife. Public support was aroused in the country for conservation of wildlife in general. It was demonstrated when people took to the streets of Delhi and Bombay to force the government to turn back Saudi hunters who wanted to hunt the great Indian bustard, a very rare, large game bird.

Project Tiger teams shifted villages from reserves. They settled the people and their livestock on new land, and ploughed it ready for their crops. Clinics, schools and even temples were

Watchtowers (above) equipped with radios help guards summon help to extinguish fires and combat poachers in tiger reserves. Records are kept of temperatures, humidity and rainfall (left).

ABOVE: Most tigers avoid people, but it is safer to travel on elephants rather than on foot in the jungle.

Tigers and leopards killed livestock; crops were ravaged by deer and monkeys; and educational and health facilities were only available outside the reserves, and at a considerable distance.

But some people found it heart-breaking to leave their homes of a lifetime. In places, villages had existed for several hundred years and people felt strong ties with the soil. Nevertheless, the government was firm that India's declining wildlife must be preserved. Reserves had to be free of human disturbance.

Relieved of the pressure of livestock grazing and cutting wood for fuel, vegetation recovered in the reserves. Small dams were built to hold water for wild animals during the hot summers, when streams often dry up. In fact, rehabilitation of the habitat improved the flow of some streams throughout the year.

In some countries, little could be done. Indo-China was convulsed by war and its aftermath. It was too late for the Caspian tiger in Iran. Conservation efforts were planned if tigers could be located, but no trace was found. China only hesitantly developed relations with the outside world in an effort to preserve its tigers.

However, the USSR had a sound tiger conservation programme. Malaysia was sufficiently properous to care for its own reserves. Nepal, Thailand and Indonesia boosted protection in their parks and sanctuaries with WWF assistance. By 1989, 20 years after the epoch-making IUCN General Assembly in Delhi, it was clear that the tiger had been given a new lease of life.

provided to compensate for the uprooting. Most villagers were happy to move. Many villages had been established relatively recently by the government to provide labour for forestry. Now that the logging had been stopped, people found it increasingly difficult to make a living.

Scientists 'shoot' tigers with special darts (top) primed with a tranquillizer. A funnel of white cloth (above) guides the tiger to the gun.

Special reserves and protection from hunting have halted the decline of the tiger in India and Nepal. But to support an active, long-term conservation programme, research is needed into the tiger's little-known way of life. What are its favourite habitat and prey? How much prey does it require? How big are its territories? Are the reserves large enough to accommodate a healthy number of tigers?

To answer some of these questions, the Smithsonian Institution of Washington DC initiated a long-term tiger ecology study by American and Nepalese scientists in the Royal Chitwan National Park in Nepal. Chitwan, bordering India at the foot of the Himalayas, was the scene of many great tiger hunts in the past. As a royal reserve it had survived the flood of people who had settled in the terai and cleared the forests. Apart from its tigers, Chitwan was one of the two largest sanctuaries left for the endangered great one-horned rhinoceros. It contained healthy populations of the whole spectrum of wildlife, which had once roamed undisturbed in the sub-Himalayan belt at a time when malaria prevented human settlement. The United Nations Development Programme (UNDP) and the Food and Agriculture Organization (FAO) provided funds and skilled advisers to help manage Chitwan and two smaller reserves to the west, Karnali-Bardia and Sukhla Phanta, where tigers survived.

In Chitwan, scientists have combined the latest techniques of wildlife research with traditional hunting practices. A buffalo bait is staked out to attract a tiger. While it is absorbed in its meal, skilled Nepalese *shikaris* (hunters) quietly draw two lengths of white cloth through the forest in the form of a letter V. The marksman, now a scientist armed with a dart gun, posts himself in a tree at the point of the V. The Nepalese hunters mount elephants and line up at its open end. At a given signal they move towards the tiger, shouting and banging gongs and sticks. The elephants rumble and trumpet, crashing through the jungle. Startled, the tiger retreats from its kill. It finds the white cloth hemming it in on both sides, and heads into the ever-narrowing V – into the sights of the scientist. Crack! The scientist fires. Instead of a bullet, a tranquillizing dart lodges in the tiger's flank. With a roar the tiger rushes off. It takes a few minutes for the tranquillizer to act. But soon the tiger falters and drops to the ground in a drugged sleep.

Scientists and hunters on their elephants locate the tiger in the undergrowth. Water is rushed up in buckets and poured over the tranquillized animal to keep it cool, because the drug can raise its temperature to fatal levels. A cloth protects the tiger's open, but unseeing, eyes from damage from dust and light.

The research team stretch tape measures from the tip of the nose to the base of the tail, and along the tail. They examine the body for injuries and collect any ticks. They check the teeth, measure the length of the canines

and remove a single incisor, which will be sectioned to determine the tiger's age. They sketch the cheek marks. These differ on every tiger and thus aid identification when the tiger is seen. The body, gathered up in a cloth, is weighed on a spring balance. Meanwhile, the neck has been measured and a collar cut to size. To it is fixed a small radio transmitter. The collar is rivetted in place. The scientist checks with his receiver whether the transmitter is working. A regular 'kissing sound'

ABOVE: Tranquillizer drugs cause a tiger's temperature to rise to dangerous levels unless its body is kept cool with water.

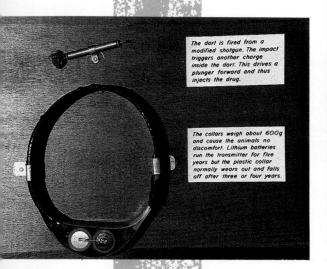

The dart is fired from a modified shotgun. The impact triggers another charge inside the dart. This drives a plunger forward and thus injects the drug.

The collars weigh about 600g and cause the animals no discomfort. Lithium batteries run the transmitter for five years but the plastic collar normally wears out and falls off after three or four years.

Tiger researcher David Smith fits a radio-collar to a tiger (above right). The collar (above) is light and fits comfortably, without affecting the tiger's movements.

reassures him. From now on, that 'beep' will enable the researchers to follow the tiger's movements.

The work is completed quickly so as not to keep the tiger tranquillized for long. Now an antidote is injected and everyone retreats. From a safe distance the scientist watches as the tiger slowly revives, blinking its eyes, showing the familiar signs of revival from an anaesthetic. It starts to rise, stumbles and collapses. Eventually, it manages to walk unsteadily away and hide in cover. There it rests. A guard watches to ensure that it is not harmed by another animal while it is still drugged.

By next morning the tiger has gone. The scientist is out with a hand antenna, listening for the signal from the radio collar. Standing on an elephant's

back he sweeps the jungle before him. The soft 'kissing' of the tiger's radio sounds in his earphones. Manoeuvring the antenna, he gets the loudest sound and notes the direction. From another point he gets a second direction and fixes the tiger's position where the lines cross. From now on this becomes a morning and evening routine as he tracks the tiger's movements. Plotted on a map, the fixes begin to show the boundaries of the tiger's range and its favoured areas.

Radio tracking revealed the tragic story of one young tiger. He was the son of Chuchchi, and about three months old when she was radio-collared. When he was about 18 months old he too was collared, so that he could be tracked as he became

independent. He was given the identi-fication number 119 (one-nineteen).

One-nineteen roamed widely in the forest. He met other tigers, but he was not powerful enough to wrest a territory from them. In a fight, his left foreleg was so severely injured that he could not straighten it. Killing wild prey became difficult and he began to starve for lack of food. The research team darted him again and treated his open wound, which healed. But he still could not straighten his leg. One-nineteen settled on the edge of the forest and survived by killing stray cattle from nearby villages.

Early one morning he climbed a river bank, and was confronted by a man on his way to bathe. He sprang on the man and killed him. People rushed up

shouting. One-nineteen fled and hid in the bushes. His beeping radio-collar enabled the researchers to capture him. There was no possibility that he could ever be free again, and he ended his days unhappily in Kathmandu's zoo.

Tracking on the ground is limited to only two or three kilometres because the radio beam travels only on line of sight. Trees and uneven ground blot out the signal. Only one or two tigers may come within range. But from the air many tigers can be located in a short time. Radio location also leads the scientist to the tiger's kills to deter-mine their age and weight. On a large deer, signs of a nape bite and a punc-tured windpipe show how the prey was killed.

ABOVE: The radio collar on this tiger can be seen as it slips through the trees in Nepal's Chitwan National Park. Scientists monitor its movements and plot its range of activity.

RIGHT: A killer tiger looked very unhappy when confined to a zoo.

Radio-collared tiger no. 119 had a crippling leg injury (left) and killed a man. He was captured and removed from the jungle on elephant back (below).

If the tiger is female, she may have cubs. They can be observed when accompanying their mother, but cannot be collared until fully grown. During several years' work, 25 tigers, as well as leopards, bears and deer, were radio-collared in Chitwan. A different frequency on each transmitter identified individuals. When mapped, the radio locations indicated the changing tiger territories. Sub-adult tigers were followed as they left their mothers and explored the forest, seeking a territory of their own.

On their daily rounds, the researchers collected tiger scats. Examined under a microscope, hairs in these droppings identified the prey on which the tiger had fed. The data collected enabled the scientific team to unfold the secret life of Chitwan's tigers, their relationships with each other, with competing carnivores such as leopards, and with prey animals.

Grasslands along the River Rapti stood out as prime tiger habitat, where the strongest tigresses made their dens and produced their cubs by a handful of powerful tigers. When a dominant tiger suddenly died in his prime, turmoil ensued as surrounding tigers battled to take over his territory.

As a result of the Chitwan study, the Nepalese government accepted the scientists' recommendations to enlarge the national park to make it more suitable for long-term conservation. The study has also provided invaluable information for improved management and conservation of tigers in other areas, although different habitats and local conditions modify tiger behaviour.

Part of the ecology study has involved putting radio-collars on the tiger's prey species to trace their movements. Tranquilliser guns are used, but deer are also captured in nets set up in a line

Scientists collect the lower jaw of a sambar prey (below) to estimate its age.

Radio-tracking helps scientists plot tiger ranges (bottom).

in the jungle. The deer are driven by a team of shouting men into the nets. Another technique is to fix a net to the ground and attach rockets to the free side. When a herd of deer comes within range, the rockets are fired so that the net falls over and traps them. They are quickly radio-collared and released.

Vegetation is the very basis of life on Earth because it converts the sun's energy into food. It is important, therefore, to know what the grazing and browsing animals feed on in a tiger area. Botanists inventory the vegetation and study its growth by fencing off plots, which are monitored over long periods. They also note what the herbivores are seen to be eating, and identify plants from analysis of the stomach contents of deer killed by tigers. Knowledge of the preferred grasses and leaves enables reserve managers to promote their growth and abundance.

Indian specialists have developed a new method of counting tigers. Tigers habitually use traditional game trails as they move through the forest. Their footprints, known as 'pugmarks', mark their passage in soft soil. Indian trackers are famous for their skill in determining whether pugmarks have been made by a male or a female – females have somewhat pointed toes on their hind feet – and in identifying individual tigers from peculiarities and injuries, just as a fingerprint expert identifies people. They can also say how recently the tiger passed that way. It was decided that, by developing these techniques, a fairly accurate tiger census was possible.

Forest guards learned to trace the shape of a fresh pugmark on to glass

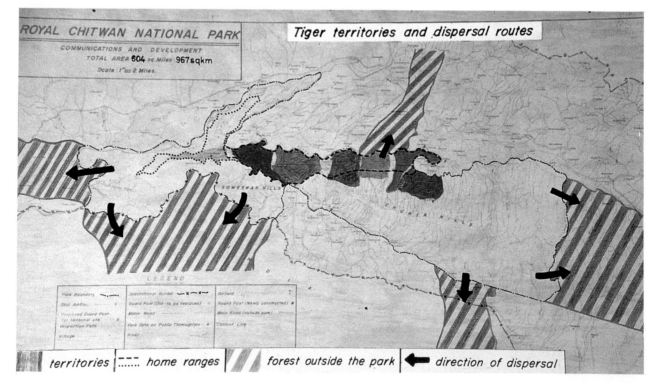

territories ······ home ranges //// forest outside the park ◀ direction of dispersal

Tiger researchers fit
a radio collar (above)
to a spotted deer, a
common tiger prey.
Measurements of
tiger pugmarks (left)
help to identify
individuals and
indicate their size.

RIGHT: Kanha Tiger
Reserve Director
Hemendra Panwar
traces the shape of
a tiger pugmark.
Each pugmark is
individually
distinctive. By
collecting tracings of
tracks in an area,
scientists are able to
estimate the number
of tigers present.

and then transfer it to a sheet of paper. When the pugmarks are very clear, the tracings can be supplemented by a plaster cast. Plaster of Paris is poured into a wooden frame placed around the pugmark. A reverse impression is obtained when it hardens.

Annual censuses are held in the tiger reserves, usually in April, during the dry season. Every five years an all-India census is held. Ten thousand forest staff and up to 100,000 volunteers go through a training course, and then move into the jungle at the appointed time. They trace fresh pugmarks and make plaster casts of the clearest ones. The place and time is noted, as well as the length of the tiger's stride, and any

ABOVE: Plaster casts of tiger tracks help identify individuals.

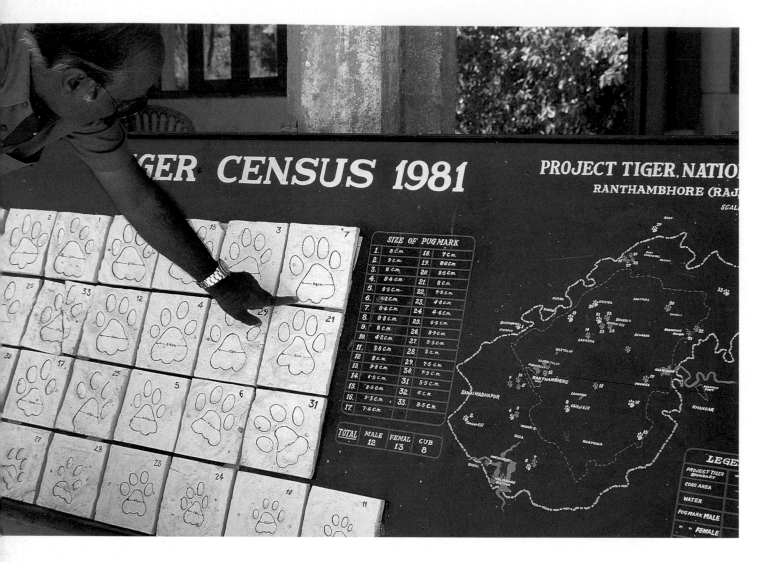

The image shows a board titled "TIGER CENSUS 1981 — PROJECT TIGER, NATIONAL RANTHAMBHORE (RAJ.)" with pugmark casts and a map.

SIZE OF PUGMARK

1.	8 c.m.	18.	7 c.m.
2.	9 c.m.	19.	8.2 c.m.
3.	8 c.m.	20.	8.5 c.m.
4.	8.4 c.m.	21.	8 c.m.
5.	6.5 c.m.	22.	7.5 c.m.
6.	5.2 c.m.	23.	4.8 c.m.
7.	8.4 c.m.	24.	4.6 c.m.
8.	8.8 c.m.	25.	6.5 c.m.
9.	8 c.m.	26.	5.9 c.m.
10.	4.2 c.m.	27.	5.5 c.m.
11.	3.8 c.m.	28.	5 c.m.
12.	8 c.m.	29.	7.5 c.m.
13.	9.8 c.m.	30.	7.5 c.m.
14.	6.5 c.m.	31.	5.5 c.m.
15.	8.5 c.m.	32.	6 c.m.
16.	9.5 c.m.	33.	8.5 c.m.
17.	7.4 c.m.		

TOTAL	MALE	FEMAL	CUB
	12	13	8

LEGEND
PROJECT TIGER BOUNDARY
CORE AREA
WATER
PUG MARK MALE
" " FEMALE

ABOVE: Reserve Director Fateh Singh Rathore shows casts of tiger pugmarks in Ranthambhore.

peculiarity in its gait. If the tiger has been seen making the tracks, its cheek stripes can sometimes be noted as well. The collected records are checked to minimize double-counting before being sent to the headquarters of Project Tiger for final analysis. Carefully done, the result produces a close estimate of the number of tigers in the country.

In a few places a check is made by counting the tigers that come to waterholes. During the dry season most of the water in the forest dries up, leaving just a few sources, where observers can be posted. It is reckoned that every tiger in the area will visit a waterhole at least once in three days. Individuals can be identified by their cheek stripes. The count can be compared with the results of the pugmark census.

Scientists at Pune (Poona) University are now applying computer analysis to pugmarks. By comparing a large number, they are locating certain points on the pads, which can be used to identify individuals, and thus ensure even more exact censuses.

TEN

PROBLEMS
AND
SOLUTIONS

ABOVE: Collection of wood for cooking fuel is depleting forests in Asia.

Tigers lived for hundreds of thousands of years in an ocean of forests, heavily populated with prey, where people existed in small numbers in isolated groups. In a few decades in this century the situation has been transformed. Now it is the tigers that live isolated in small numbers. An ocean of people has replaced the ocean of trees and is pressing in on the remaining islands of tiger habitat. Tiger prey is equally under siege.

The human population explosion in the twentieth century resulted from improved medical treatment and technological advances in industry and agriculture. The world population of 5,234 million represents as much as 10 per cent of all who have ever lived on Earth in the last 10,000 years. Human feet have trodden the highest summits and reached the most remote and wild lands. Despite all controls, the human population will continue to grow for several decades yet. The increase will be mainly in the developing countries, where most of the remaining wild lands lie.

To support humankind, the natural resources of the Earth are being strained by the spread of mining, fishing, agriculture and forest exploitation. Rivers are dammed and diverted; wetlands are drained. Tropical moist forests originally covered 4,300,000 km² (1,660,000 sq. miles) from India through southeast Asia. More than half has already been cleared. By the end of the century, at least a further 200,000 km² (77,200 sq. miles) are likely to disappear. Apart from clearance for agriculture, well over half the wood is cut for firewood, the only source of energy available to tens of millions of Asians, and for building material. The remainder goes to developed countries, especially Japan. The consequences for all wildlife are obvious. And the tiger, which lives at the top of the food chain, will be among those that fare worst. Fragmentation of forests into islands surrounded by agriculture isolates tigers, which will not cross open land.

Scientists calculate that a contiguous population of at least 500 tigers is needed to maintain full species evolutionary potential. In other words, that is the minimum number needed in any one area to maintain the genetic ability to adapt to a changing environment. Only in the Sundarbans mangrove forests does this condition clearly exist. Most other reserves in the Indian subcontinent hold fewer than 100 tigers. Some reserves are still linked by belts of forest. Unfortunately, these forest corridors are threatened by the pressure for agricultural land.

Tigers exist in large tracts of continuous forest in Burma and parts of southeast Asia, but their numbers are not known. Again the forests there are being cleared and tigers isolated. To counter the ill-effects of inbreeding in small, isolated populations, the translocation of just one unrelated breeding animal in each generation is sufficient. If tigers are moved around a group of reserves, it makes them the equivalent of a much larger, and therefore genetically healthier, tiger population.

Reserves themselves are subject to the destructive pressures of cattle grazing and wood collection. There are too few guards. And those few are usually miserably under-equipped and under-paid, struggling to keep the human waves at bay. Local people often have good reason to resent the protected areas. Formerly, they could graze their livestock there, and collect wood and other products. That has been stopped. Outside the reserves, cattle and goats have often turned grazing lands to near desert. Demand for firewood for cooking and heating has devastated wooded areas. Within the reserves people can see lush grasses and forests of useful wood. Moreover, the reserves are sanctuaries for animals that emerge at night to ravage crops, and sometimes injure and kill people. It is no wonder that conflict arises between people and protected areas.

The Indian tiger reserve of Ranthambhore is a case in point. It consists of 500 km² (193 sq. miles) of rocky hills covered with light forest intersected by luxuriant valleys, near the eastern edge of the Rajasthan desert. Ruined fortresses and palaces bear testimony to centuries of human occupation. When it was declared a tiger reserve in 1973,

Coastal mangroves in the Sundarbans are home to tigers and their spotted deer prey (above right). Many forests elsewhere are doomed because seedlings are grazed by goats and cattle (above).

some villages still existed inside it. To improve the integrity of the reserve, the people were moved out, given good agricultural land and helped to rebuild their village communities.

But the life-giving monsoon is a fickle visitor to this part of India. Many years it fails and there is little or no rain to promote the regeneration of crops and grazing land. Some 50,000 cattle and 50,000 goats belonging to 66 villages around the park need fodder. Inevitably, the villagers want to send them into the reserve, where the grass grows tall. Battles have developed between guards and villagers, in which at least 15 forest guards, including the director, and some village people have been injured since 1980. Graziers have

even built roadblocks to prevent guards reaching areas where they have been illegally grazing their cattle.

During a severe drought in 1986, thousands of cattle entered Ranthambhore. Armed police were despatched to drive out cattle and graziers. Last year a tiger killed a child. Such episodes only increase the bitter conflict between people and the reserve. Ranthambhore is probably one of the best protected reserves in India, possibly in Asia. Even so, a recent study found that 126 of the 157 compartments into which the reserve is divided were affected by illegal grazing, and 86 by wood poaching.

Wildlife authorities know that they need the understanding and support of local people, but they are often handicapped because they have no authority or funds to operate outside reserves. There is insufficient cooperation from other wings of government.

A private Ranthambhore Foundation is now trying to relieve pressure on the reserve by improving facilities for local people. The foundation provides mobile clinics for health care and family planning, and high-grade cattle to improve local breeds and milk production. These cattle can be stall-fed instead of being sent out to graze. Experts are helping to rehabilitate village grazing lands, which have been destroyed by over-use. Village children learn about the wildlife in their neighbourhood and visit the reserve. If the programme is successful, it will be extended to other reserves. Furthermore, it can be hoped that, once governments have seen what can be

achieved, they will undertake similar schemes.

In Nepal, the government is already taking action. Local people are allowed into the Chitwan National Park for two weeks each year to collect the tall grass for thatch and fodder. Outside they cannot get sufficient supplies because of excessive grazing by their cattle and goats.

Wildlife tourism helps to promote conservation, but it has become a problem in popular viewing areas. People from all over the world now want to see tigers, which, protected by Project Tiger, have become bold and visible in a few reserves. Urban Indians, who formerly had little interest in their country's wildlife, visit the reserves in increasing numbers. At peak times, in the early mornings and in the evenings, tourist traffic in prime areas of Ranthambhore has become

BELOW: Ruined palaces and fortresses add to the charm of Ranthambhore Tiger Reserve, 200 km (120 miles) south of Delhi.

intense. Too many vehicles disturb wildlife, including tigers, and damage forest tracks. Tourist numbers and entry times in Ranthambhore and other popular reserves are now being limited.

Poaching is another constant threat. The tiger has legal protection in all countries of its range, except Burma. International commerce in any part of a tiger has been banned since 1976 by the Convention on International Trade in Endangered Species of Wild Fauna and Flora (CITES). Anti-fur movements in western Europe and North America have reduced demand for skins. Nevertheless, clandestine trade continues to encourage poaching. The principal markets for tiger skins are Arabian countries, Taiwan and Japan.

Western tourists still conceal skins in luggage, seldom checked by customs. From time to time, illegal hoards of tiger skins are uncovered by the authorities. Increased vigilance and firm action, with public support, are required to reduce poaching and illegal trade to a minimum.

China has few tigers left to provide bones for popular medicines, but appears to be getting supplies from other Asian countries. In Taiwan, the public slaughter of tigers for gourmet meat caused an international scandal in 1984. Tigers have never existed in Taiwan, and, after the scandal, the government clamped down on imports.

People in developed countries support tiger conservation but the prob-

BELOW: India's tiger reserves attract large numbers of local tourists. In the delta region of the Sundarbans, where tigers are aggressive, they may only land in protected places.

Name of Paper :
NATIONAL HERALD
Date , NEW DELHI
25 MAR 1988

Animal skin worth crores seized

Herald News Service
NEW DELHI, March 24 —
The Delhi Police on Thursda
seized skins of several anima
which were being treated in
house in Jafarabad in th
Seelampur area of East Delh
The seizure is worth crores c
rupees in the internationa
market.

Three persons Maqboo
Abdul Rashid and Siddiqi c
Kashmir, were arrested from th
house.

Police said that the SHO of th
Seelampur police station ha
been tipped off that the skins c
various animals and reptile
were being treated in a hous
which had been taken on rent b
Sansar Chand of Bara Tooti i
the walled city area.

A party, led by the SHO
raided the house and found th
three treating various skin wit
salt and chemicals.

Among the seized skins wer
25,000 skins of snakes, 2,000 o
jackals, 500 of jungle cats, 700 o
fox and red fox, one of a tige
which was 12 feet long, six o
leopards and one of a wolf.

The kingpin of the racket, San
sar Chand, is absconding an
police said that he had bee
arrested on the same charg
some time ago and was freed o
the orders of the High Cour
where the case is being pursued.

The arrests were made unde
the Wildlife Protection Act
1972.

opard skins seized during a raid by East Delhi Police in the Jafarabad locality being displayed at the
elampur police post on Thursday. —Herald photo by Kishore Kamboj.

Name of Paper : Patriot
Published : New Delhi
Date : 1 APR 1

Anithal skins worth Rs 30 lakh seized

More than 5,000 pieces of skins
of animals worth Rs 30 lakh in
the international market were
seized by the personnel of the
Wildlife Department of the
Delhi Administration on
Thursday, reports PTI.

The seizure of skins belonging to valuable and endangered
species like fox-cats, snow-fox
and domestic cats was made
from a godown of a transport
company in north Delhi, according to wildlife officer D P
Dwivedi.

He said the consignment
was booked from Nagai in
Rajasthan to Delhi. However,
there were no arrests.

Name of Paper : Patriot
Published : New Delhi
Date : 15 OCT 1987

Tigers: Poachers trading in
prized animal skins have killed at

least 50 al Bengal tigers by
poisoning Bangladesh in the
past yea a government-run
newspape said on Tuesday.

Forestry officials told the
"Dainir Janata" newspaper that
rangers found the skinned tigers
deep in the Sundarbans forest.

LEFT: Wildlife authorities fight a constant battle with poachers and illegal traders in animal skins and bones. Demand for them continues in some parts of the world.

lems are not theirs. Tiger attacks on livestock or local people breed resentment and opposition to conservation of dangerous animals. Villagers poison tigers which become a nuisance. The question: 'Are tigers more important than people?' is raised, not only at local levels, but at the national level after a spate of attacks, or if villages are moved from reserves. In one incident, when a man was killed by a tiger, his friends began shouting at the guards: 'You're not trying to catch that tiger. You don't care about us. If we kill a tiger we go to prison, but if a tiger kills one of us, nobody cares. We are just dogs'. However, when the tiger was captured, there was jubilation and the overt anger abated.

Sympathy for the problems of people living close to tigers arouses concern among a wider community. Indian newspapers challenge any over-emphasis on saving tigers to the detriment of people. Such adverse public reactions worry conservationists, because the future of the tiger, and all potentially dangerous wildlife, depends on public support. Wildlife authorities thus face the challenge of placating people, while saving tigers.

In Kheri District, near India's border with western Nepal, where there has been an epidemic of tiger attacks around the Dudhwa National Park, tiger specialists say the trouble has arisen because sugarcane is grown up to the very edge of the park. They

ABOVE: A woman seeks a prescription in Hong Kong. Chinese have traditionally used animal parts, including tiger bones, as medicine.

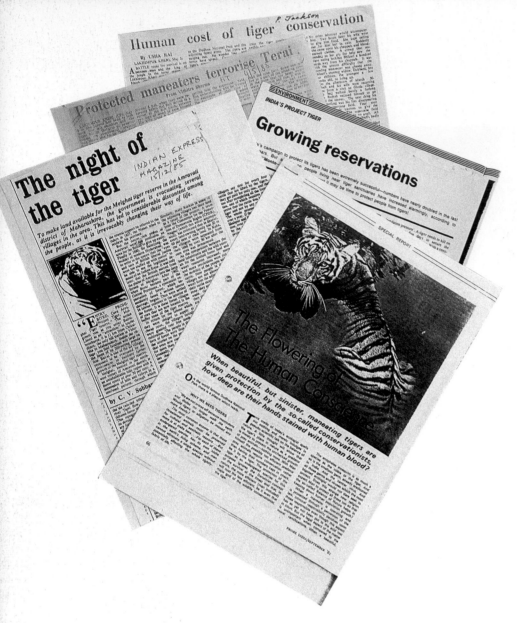

ABOVE: India is proud of its success in conserving its famous tigers. But there are still problems for people who live close to them.

want sugarcane cultivation near the park banned. But local farmers do not want to give up this highly profitable crop. Controls on grazing and firewood collection are also proposed. People are urged to work in groups, which are less likely to be attacked by tigers than lone individuals. Tiger Watch teams have been ordered to follow the movements of tigers in the area, and to deal with any incipient problems. Tigresses with cubs are provided with baits positioned so as to draw them back to the park. If necessary, a tiger may be trapped and removed to a zoo. Some have been shot.

The family of anyone killed receives compensation. Farmers are also compensated for loss of livestock, provided that it was not inside the reserve.

Some local people argue that tigers are welcome because they keep deer and pigs out of their crops. In an area of Sumatra, where wild pigs proliferated after elimination of the tigers which preyed on them, a farmer said he no longer informed the authorities if he found signs of tigers, because he feared that they would be hunted down for trophies.

Wildlife authorities in India are confident that an occasional outcry against tigers will not affect the tiger conservation programme. Even in politically turbulent West Bengal, where legislators have from time to time aroused passions over the human toll in the Sundarbans, governments of all persuasions, including Communist, have stood firmly in support of conserving the Sundarbans and its tigers. They have evicted people who have tried to settle in the reserve.

Hemendra Panwar, director of the Wildlife Institute of India, has played a leading role in both tiger conservation and improving the lot of local people. He declares: 'Our programme is not just for the tiger. It aims at conserving whole ecosystems, consisting mainly of forests, which are of vital importance to human welfare. The tiger is an important component of these ecosystems. Despite the occasional incidents of man-killing – and there have been only a small number outside the Sundarbans and Kheri – the programme must go on because it is in the larger interests of humanity.'

ELEVEN

CAN THE TIGER SURVIVE?

ABOVE: If tigers are to survive, there must be flourishing numbers of their prey animals, such as swamp deer, seen here with the very rare wild buffalo.

'Of the many ways of measuring a land's wealth, one of the surest signs of ecological richness and diversity is an abundance of predator species. Because each species sits at the top of a different food chain, belonging to a different cycle of organic matter, we can be certain of the existence of a larger animal community for every predator. This is, in turn, sustained by vegetation. The existence of carnivores carries the implications of a larger ecological community and of millions of years of evolutionary struggle.'
Jonathan Kingdon, *East African Mammals*, Vol. IIIa (Academic Press 1977).

Tigers, like people, can only exist if they have sufficient food. In the case of the tiger, as of all carnivores, that food consists of other wild animals. A tiger requires about a hundred large prey every year. It follows that a genetically healthy tiger population of 500 tigers needs up to 50,000 large prey. To produce sufficient young to sustain such an off-take, a total population of 500,000 prey animals is required. They, in turn, are dependent on plants – palatable grasses, leaves and shoots. All require an adequate supply of water and sufficient living space. The health of the ecological community also involves many other species, which form

part of the working 'machine' of nature. Birds spread seeds. Carrion eaters and insects break down dead matter and return the nutrients to the soil. These nutrients, essential to all life, are recycled through the living community. The whole provides a balanced world ecosystem into which the human race fits.

Between 6,000 and 9,000 tigers roam the forests of 12 countries in Asia today. They represent only a tiny relic of the numbers which once spread from Turkey in the west to the Sea of Okhotsk in the Far East. The decline has been mainly in our present century, during which the human population has more than quadrupled to over 5,000 million. The increase has largely been in the developing countries, which includes the tiger's habitat through south and southeast Asia. Natural areas, never before disturbed, have had to be converted to living space and agriculture to produce food for the billions.

Large wild animals are in future, likely to be confined to reserves. Outside them their prospects are poor. But the scope for more and larger reserves is rapidly decreasing. Moreover, tigers and other large predators, which are always relatively few in number, may face genetic decline and ultimate extinction through inbreeding when

ABOVE: India has 17 tiger reserves, including Dudhwa National Park on the border with Nepal, where wildlife flourishes.

LEFT: The Siberian tiger is the most powerfully built of all the tiger subspecies. It tolerates harsh winters, when the snow is deep and temperatures sink to minus 50°C (minus 58° F). Known in China as the Manchurian or Northeast China tiger, its coat is thicker and paler than that of other tigers, and its stripes are brown instead of black. Fewer than 300 survive in the wild, but there are over 600 in zoos all over the world.

LEFT: All forest guards in India receive special training in the care of wildlife.

confined to small areas, unless mankind comes to their aid. Ideally, forest corridors should link reserves so that as many animals as possible can interbreed. That is not always possible. To maintain the gene pool, it will be necessary to translocate some animals between reserves.

Scientific breeding of threatened species is being increasingly attempted to ensure maximum genetic variability in the captive population. The Siberian tiger, which is a prime example, now numbers over 600 in captivity – about twice the number in the wild. Captive-bred antelope and deer have been successfully reintroduced to the wild, but reintroducing large captive-bred carnivores to the wild is fraught with difficulties. They need parental training in capturing prey. They may continue to try to be familiar with

people. This can be alarming, and might lead to accidents. Adverse public reaction can hamper conservation efforts.

The only answer is to maintain an adequate network of reserves. But, for this, an enormous investment in funds and people is required. The funds must be sufficient to provide guards to protect tigers and other wild animals; managers to ensure habitat protection and monitor the wildlife; and scientists to investigate the requirements of various species and make recommendations for management. Political will and international support are required for such a big programme.

In the past 20 years, the tiger has become a symbol of wildlife conservation, its successes, and its problems. Its continued life on Earth challenges us all.

TIGER IN INDIA				Density						LEOPARD
STATES RESERVES	AREA KM²	1984 STATES	1984 RESERVES	1984 KM²/TIGER	1979/80 STATES	1979/80 RESERVES	1977 RESERVES	1972 STATES	1972 RESERVES	1984 RESERVES
ANDHRA PRADESH		164			148			35		
Nagarjunasagar	3000		65	46						
ARUNACHAL		219			139			69		
PRADESH Namdapha	1808		43	42						40
ASSAM		376			300			147		
Manas	2840		123	23		69	105		31	
BIHAR		138			74			85		
Palamau	930		62	15		37	26		22	
GUJARAT		9			7			8		
HARYANA		1								
KARNATAKA		202			156			102		
Bandipur	690		53	13		39	26		10	43
KERALA		89			134			60		
Periyar	777		44	18		34				
MADHYA PRADESH		786			579			457		
Indrawati	2084		38	55						
Kanha	1984		109	18		71	55		43	74
MAHARASHTRA		301			160			160		
Melghat	1571		80	20		63	57		27	50
MANIPUR		6			10			1		
MEGHALAYA		125			35			32		
MIZORAM		33			65			0		
NAGALAND		104			102			80		
ORISSA		202			173			142		
Simlipal	2750		71	39		65	60		77	67
RAJASTHAN		96			79			74		
Ranthambhor	392		38	10		25	22		14	40
Sariska	800		26	31		19				
SIKKIM		2								
TAMILNADU		97			65			33		
Mundanthurai	567									
TRIPURA		5			6			7		
UTTAR PRADESH		698			487			262		
Corbett	520		90	6		84	73		44	43
Dudhwa	811									
WEST BENGAL		352			296			73		
Buxar	745		15	50						
Sunderbans	2585		264	10		205	181		50	
TOTALS STATES		4005			3015			1827		
RESERVES	24854		1121			711	605		318	357
TIGER IN NEPAL 1985										
Royal Chitwan NP	1040		60	18		100	11			
Royal Bardia WS	1336		100	14						
Royal Sukhlaphant WS	1355		50	28		75	19			
TOTALS	3731		210	275						

WORLD TIGER POPULATION

COUNTRY	MINIMUM	MAXIMUM
PANTHERA TIGRIS TIGRIS		
Bangladesh	400	600
Bhutan	150	250
Burma	200	300
India	3500	4500
Nepal	200	300
TOTAL	*4450*	*5950*
PANTHERA TIGRIS ALTAICA		
USSR	200	350
China	30	50
Korea	?	?
TOTAL	*230*	*400*
PANTHERA TIGRIS AMOYENSIS		
China	30	50
PANTHERA TIGRIS SUMATRAE		
Indonesia	500	1000
PANTHERA TIGRIS CORBETTI		
Burma	200	300
Kampuchea	?	?
Laos	?	?
Malaysia	560	620
Thailand	400	600
Vietnam	?	?
TOTAL	*1160*	*1520*
GRAND TOTAL	*6370*	*8920*

ZOO POPULATIONS
(Studbook registrations)

P.T. TIGRIS	19m/23f	42	31/12/87
ALTAICA	297m/363f	660	31/12/87
AMOYENSIS	33m/18f	51	31/12/87
SUMATRAE	64m/81f	145	31/12/87
CORBETTI	3.2	5	31/12/84
(some corbetti in Chinese zoos)			

TIGER RESERVES IN INDIA

INDEX

SELECT BIBLIOGRAPHY

The literature on tigers is vast. The following represents only a small selection.

Bragin, A. P. 1986. Population Characteristics and Social-Spatial Patterns of the Tiger on the Eastern Macroslope of the Sikhote-Alin Mountain Range, USSR. Academy of Sciences of the USSR.

Courtney, Nicholas. 1980. *The Tiger: Symbol of Freedom*. Quartet.

Gee, E. P. 1964. *The Wildlife of India*. Collins.

Guggisberg, C. A. W. 1975. *Wild Cats of the World*. David and Charles.

Leyhausen, Paul. 1979. *Cat Behaviour: The Predatory and Social Behaviour of Domestic and Wild Cats*. Garland.

Locke, Lt. Col. A. 1954. *The Tigers of Trengganu*. Museum Press.

McDougal, Charles. 1977. *The Face of the Tiger*. Rivington Books and Andre Deutsch.

McNeely, Jeffrey A. and Paul Spencer Wachtel. 1988. *The Soul of the Tiger*. Doubleday.

Matjushkin, E. N., V. I. Zhyvotchenko and E. N. Smirnov. 1980. *The Amur Tiger in the USSR*. International Union for Conservation of Nature and Natural Resources (IUCN).

Mountfort, Guy. 1981. *Saving the Tiger*. Michael Joseph/Viking.

National Wildlife Federation. 1987. *Kingdom of Cats*. National Wildlife Federation.

Perry, Richard. 1964. *The World of the Tiger*. Cassell and Company.

Prater, S. H. 1965. *The Book of Indian Animals*. Bombay Natural History Society.

Project Tiger, India. 1979. International Symposium on Tiger, February 22–24, 1979. Government of India, Dept of Environment.

Sankhala, Kailash S. 1978. *Tiger!* Rupa/Collins.

Schaller, George S. 1967. *The Deer and the Tiger*. University of Chicago Press.

Seidensticker, John and Md Abdul Hai. 1983. *The Sundarbans Wildlife Management Plan: Conservation in the Bangladesh Coastal Zone*. International Union for Conservation of Nature and Natural Resources (IUCN).

Seidensticker, John and Ir. Suyono. 1980. *The Javan Tiger and the Meru Betiri Reserve: A Plan for Management*. International Union for Conservation of Nature and Natural Resources (IUCN).

Shuker, Karl P. N. 1989. *Mystery Cats of the World*. Robert Hale.

Singh, Arjan. 1981. *Tara, a Tigress*. Quartet.

Singh, Arjan. 1984. *Tiger! Tiger!* Jonathan Cape.

Sunquist, Mel and Fiona. 1988. *Tiger Moon*. University of Chicago Press.

Sunquist, Melvin E. 1981. *The Social Organization of Tigers in Royal Chitwan National Park, Nepal*. Smithsonian Contributions to Zoology, No. 336.

Thapar, Valmik. 1986. *Tiger: Portrait of a Predator*. Collins.

Thapar, Valmik. 1989. *Tigers: The Secret Life*. Elm Tree Books.

Tilson, Ronald L. and Ulysses S. Seal. 1987. *Tigers of the World: The Biology, Management and Conservation of an Endangered Species*. Noyes Publications.

Toovey, Jacqueline (editor). 1987. *Tigers of the Raj: The Shikar Diaries of Colonel Burton*. Alan Sutton.

Zozayong. 1977. *Korean Folk Painting*. Emillle Museum.